The Little
STYLE GUIDE
to Great Christian
Writing and Publishing

The Little
STYLE GUIDE
to Great Christian
Writing and Publishing

Leonard G. Goss
& Carolyn Stanford Goss

BROADMAN
&HOLMAN
PUBLISHERS

Nashville, Tennessee

0-8054-2787-2

Published by Broadman & Holman Publishers
Nashville, Tennessee

Dewey Classification Number: 808
Subject Heading: AUTHORSHIP—STYLE MANUALS
\ CHRISTIAN LITERATURE—TECHNIQUE

1 2 3 4 5 6 7 8 9 10 08 07 06 05 04

Dedicated with love to Edward, Paul, Charles,
Philip, Sara, Cheryl, Cindy, and Shawn.
Our brothers and sisters, our friends.

Contents

Preface and Acknowledgments

This little style guide is meant to help writers and editors and all those involved in Christian publishing contribute to clarity of communication and ease and speed of comprehension. We hope it will help produce books that provide a fresh understanding and a distinctively Christian examination of questions confronting readers in their personal lives, families, churches, communities, and the wider culture. Although these qualities are expressed in different ways in different kinds of literature, we want to make these general characteristics a central part of both the fiction and nonfiction that is published.

Steve Bond, Lawrence Kimbrough, John Landers, Victoria Lee, Lisa Parnell, and Gail Rothwell made up the advisory committee for *The Little Style Guide to Great Christian Writing and Publishing*. Many thanks to them for their encouragement, expertise, and advice. As our editor on this book, Steve Bond has taken on a double-dose of responsibility, and he honors us by being our in-house sponsor at Broadman & Holman Publishers. Kim Overcash has been a very pleasant and effective project editor for this book, and we thank her sincerely for all her help. We also want to give thanks to friends and colleagues for all they do to make a difference in the publishing world: Jennifer Allison, Susanne Anhalt, Angela Baker, Ed Barber, Lila Bishop, Cecil Boswell, Pam Braswell, Courtney Brooks, Sheila Brown, Trent Butler, Brenda Cain, Jill Carter, Vicki Catoe, David Chandler, Ray Clendenen, Susan Dawson, Michael DeMonico, Laura Dunkley, Jean Eckenrode, Samantha Escue, Janell Fadler, Sue Farmer, Sherry Featherston, Pat Fields, Reagan Frazier, Sam Gantt, Michelle Garcia, Sharon Gilbert, Martha Goostree, Ted Griffin, Tim Grubbs, Michael Harris, Rena Harris, Steve Hawkins, Judi Hayes, Deann Hebert, Larry Herbert, Stephanie Huffman, Heather Hulse, Lisa Jennette, Don Johnson, Ricky King, Chris Koffman, Kevin Kunce, Diana Lawrence, Nicole Lee, Brandi Lewis, Robert Loftin, Amber Mackie, Rick Maurer, Jennifer McAfee, Dewayne McFarlin, Bill McNatt, Paul Mikos, Trish Morrison, Sheila Moss, Misty Moyer, Lloyd Mullins, Rod Murphree, John Nehlig, Steve Nesmith, David O'Brien, Robin Patterson, Bill Polk, Gregory Pope, Elizabeth Randle, Pat Reynolds, Dean Richardson, Freddie Rivera, Sherry Rodriquez, Emily Ryan, Larry Sanborn, David Schrader, Mary Beth Shaw, Shemika Small, Carole Smith, David Stabnow, Matt Stewart, Nancy Temple, Gary Terashita, Paula Thomas, John Thompson, Zan Tyler, Pamela Ufen, Thomas Walters, Brenda West, Matt West, Carie Whitaker, Kay Whitley, Pam Wiley, Sharon Wiley, George Williams, David Woodard, and Kathy Zeigler. We gratefully acknowledge our appreciation for the opportunity to share with them in publishing serious books that help writers and readers be salt and light in society. In addition, we are indebted to Ted Griffin for sharing his thoughts on the editor-author relationship.

We must not forget to express our appreciation to Jimmy Draper, David Shepherd, Ken Stephens, and Ted Warren for their oversight, encouragement, and counsel. We heartily thank them all for being devoted to publishing good books and for leading the vision that lies behind our publishing model and our work together to strike blows for the Kingdom.

Soli Deo Gloria.

LGG   CSG

Introduction

Each section of *The Little Style Guide to Great Christian Writing and Publishing* includes a parenthetical cross-reference to additional information and examples to be found in *The Chicago Manual of Style, Fifteenth Edition* (Chicago: The University of Chicago Press, 2003). The *CMS* is the really essential guide all writers, editors, and proofreaders must have. In those cases that may be ambiguous, however, remember that this style guide is addressed to the unique problems of religious writers and writing.

Our authorities for spelling and usage are the unabridged *Webster's Third New International Dictionary of the English Language* and its latest abridged form, *Merriam-Webster's Collegiate Dictionary, Eleventh Edition* (2003). When we have needed an example from the New Testament to illustrate a point, we have used *The Holman Christian Standard Bible* (Nashville: Holman Bible Publishers, 2001).

CHAPTER 1
Book Production

A. Preparation of the Manuscript
(2.3–.46)

1. It is the author's responsibility to provide copy (disk and printout) that is clear, readable, and accurate. The manuscript must be typed and double-spaced. It should have wide margins (1 inch) on good quality standard white bond paper 8 1/2 x 11 inches. Computer printouts should preferably be printed by a laser printer. Colored paper or flimsy onionskin is not acceptable, for it is soon reduced to tatters in the editorial office. Print only one side of the paper.

2. The manuscript must be complete. Additions and corrections are confusing and difficult to add once the manuscript has been accepted for publication. The author should include the following parts with the book:

> Title Page
> Table of Contents
> All text matter
> Footnotes on separate pages, at end of book,
>   not in a running footnotes window

      Tables or graphs on separate pages
      Bibliography
      Indexes (prepared by author after final proofs
        are available)

3. The manuscript pages should be numbered consecutively in the upper *right* corner. Do *not* number them by chapter (3–1, 3–2, etc.). Sheets inserted after the manuscript has been paginated should carry the preceding page number with *a, b, c* added: *86a, 86b, 86c.* If a page is later removed, the preceding page should be double numbered: 106–7.

4. It is the author's responsibility to check all Scripture references, quotations, and footnotes for accuracy prior to submitting the manuscript.

5. All books must be sent on a 3.5 inch disk, in Microsoft Word or a program compatible with it. The disk must be Macintosh or IBM compatible.

B. Rights and Permissions (4.11–.98)

1. The publisher will prepare the copyright page and also has the privilege to give permission to reprint excerpts in other publications.

2. If the author wishes to use a portion of a copyrighted work and there is some question whether the kind or amount of the material exceeds a fair use, the author should request permission to quote the portion in question. It is the author's responsibility to obtain permission to quote from other sources. Notice of the original copyright and permission to reprint must appear either on the copyright page of the book or in a footnote on the first page of the reprinted material or in a special list of

acknowledgments. All permissions or copies of them must be sent to the publisher.

3. The author is further responsible for any fees charged by grantors of permission unless the author makes other arrangements with the grantor. When the publisher pays the cost of procuring permission rights, the publisher generally deducts these costs from the author's future royalties.

4. Frequent use of modern Scripture versions may require permission.

C. Stages in Manuscript Production (2.50, 3.43)

1. An edited manuscript usually passes through the following stages in the production process:

> Sample page and design
> Typesetting
> First proofs (copy sent to author)
> Second and additional proofs (if necessary)
> Final proofs
> Camera copy
> Platemaking
> Press
> Binding

2. Once page proofs (final proofs) are made, revisions are costly and should be minimal. Major changes at this stage in production are not acceptable. Corrections should be confined to substantive errors.

3. Authors will receive final proofs *only* if the book requires an index. In this case, the author will receive a deadline to complete the index, but manuscript revisions are not made at this time.

D. The Editor-Author Relationship

1. During the editorial process, editors work with authors to produce books that are as excellent as they can be, in terms of both content and quality. Editing is usually done on screen—sometimes only for house style, sometimes in a more comprehensive way, depending on the specific needs of a given manuscript.

2. As editors edit an assigned book, they typically correct misspellings, punctuation errors, and incorrect word usage, and generally conform the book to house style. The editor also identifies and, in cooperation with the author, clarifies unclear writing, theological or historical inaccuracies, and potentially offensive material.

3. Some see the editor as a supercritical, academic-monastic individual who cackles as he edits a manuscript so heavily that writers can't recognize their own work. Others idealize the editor as a knight in shining armor who will rescue a manuscript (or an author) from obscurity, make the work great, and bring huge success! The truth is somewhere in between.

In Christian publishing, the editor and the writer have the same goals and serve the same Lord, but they are coming to the task from different angles. This sometimes makes for a nebulous world in which the rules seem unclear. Ideally, author and editor will maintain a context of cooperation and teamwork, and within that context the editor fills necessary roles on behalf of both the publisher and the author. The editor and the writer are coworkers.

Throughout the editorial process the editor gives honest feedback and offers constructive criticism. If some elements in the book do not work, are offensive to the intended readership, are theologically questionable or simply unclear, it is the editor's responsibility to work with the author to resolve the problem.

Trust is at the core of the editor-author relationship. The editor respects the writer's point of view, the purpose for the book, the style, and so on, and thus doesn't make the book the editor's rather than the writer's. On the other hand, the writer trusts the editor to tell him what the book is really like and what its strengths and weaknesses are. The editor helps a writer focus on a reading audience, on the purpose for writing the book, and on whether the story line, tone, writing flow and style, content, and vocabulary effectively reach intended readers. The editor helps the author remember that quality is just as important as content.

CHAPTER 2
Punctuation

A. Period (6.13–.17)

1. Use a period without parentheses after numerals or letters in a vertical listing.

1.	a.
2.	b.
3.	c.

2. Enclose numerals or letters in a list within a paragraph in double parentheses, or use an end parenthesis after a numeral or letter. Do not follow them with a period in either case.

> Some of the earliest texts of the New Testament have been found in (1) Oxyrhynchus Papyrus 657, (2) Chester Beatty Papyrus II, and (3) Bodmer Papyrus II.

3. Omit the period after running heads, centered headlines, and signatures.

4. Place periods within quotation marks.

> Professor Joseph's favorite saying was "There is no such thing as a dumb question."

> The would-be theologian took up residence in a cave, thinking he would thus avoid succumbing to 'the social gospel.'

B. Exclamation Point (6.76–.79)

1. Use the exclamation point to mark an emphatic or sarcastic comment.

> How beautiful is the girl in my arms!
>
> He seems to enjoy being miserable!

2. Place the exclamation within quotation marks, parentheses, or brackets when it is part of the quoted or parenthetical material; otherwise, place it outside the quotation marks.

> "Don't hang me," cried the captured rustler, "I'm innocent!"
>
> The traitor betrayed everyone, including his "friends"!

C. Question Mark (6.70–.75)

1. The question mark is used to pose a question or to express an editorial doubt.

> What is the sound of one hand clapping?
>
> *How will this affect my future?* he was thinking.
>
> The translation of the Bible made by Miles Coverdale (1488?–1569) was used to a great extent by the translators of the 1611 Authorized Version.

2. Questions within a sentence that consist of single words, such as *who, when, how,* or *why* do not require a question mark. It is better to italicize the word.

> The question is not *how* but *when*.

3. Place the question mark inside quotation marks, parentheses, or brackets when it is part of the quoted or parenthetical material.

> "Barry, did you tell your music director that you love to sing?"

4. Place the question mark outside the quotation marks when the quoted material is not a question.

> When you finish work, will you hear Jesus say, "Well done"?

5. When a question is a rhetorical one that is not meant to elicit information but is made as a more striking substitute for a statement, it does not always require a question mark. Depending on the context, it can end with a period, a comma, or even an exclamation point.

> "Who in the world would send a vampire novel to B&H!" Kim was obviously exasperated.

6. Indirect questions do not require a question mark.

> Gary asked if he could go to the writing conference.

D. Comma (6.18–.56)

A comma is used to indicate the smallest pause in continuity of thought or sentence structure. The modern practice is to pause infrequently, especially if the meaning is clear without an interruption. Aside from a few set rules, its use is a matter of good judgment.

1. Use a comma before the conjunction uniting two parts of a compound sentence unless both parts are very short.

> Carol's biscotti are pretty good, but her zwieback is the best in the county.

> Trent drove to Borders and he walked to Corky's Barbecue.

2. Use commas to set off an adjectival phrase or clause that is nonrestrictive and could be dropped without changing the reference of the noun.

> The apostle Paul, a peace-loving man, was often the target of violence from nonbelievers during his ministry.

3. Use commas to set off interjecting transitional adverbs and similar elements that effect a distinct break in the continuity of thought.

> All people of goodwill, therefore, must remain vigilant.

4. In most cases, it is best to set off a word, phrase, or clause in apposition to a noun.

> One of his brothers, Edward, is a senior partner in a well-respected law firm.

If, however, the appositive has a restrictive function, do not set it off by a comma.

> His son David is a starving actor.

5. Set off two or more adjectives by commas if each one modifies the noun alone.

> Timothy proved himself to be an honest, hardworking servant.

Exception: If the first adjective modifies the idea expressed by the combination of the second adjective and the noun, no comma is needed.

> The hungry old tiger licked his chops when he saw the missionary stumble into the clearing.

[One method to determine this usage is to ask if the word *and* can be inserted between the two modifiers without changing the meaning of the sentence or making it awkward. If it cannot, no comma is required.]

6. In a series of three or more elements, place a comma before the conjunction.

> According to legend, Vladimir studied Islam, Judaism, and Roman Catholicism before deciding to become a Christian.

7. Use commas to set off words identifying a title or position after a name.

> Nero, the cruel and bloodthirsty emperor who murdered Christians, was also responsible for the burning of Rome.

8. Use commas to indicate the date and to set off names of geographical places.

> May 30, 1949 (Alternate style: 30 May 1949)

> He was born on December 31, 1947, in San Diego, California, and later moved to Arizona.

9. Usually it is preferable to set off a dependent clause that precedes the main clause by a comma.

> If you go to the store, please get some bananas.

10. In most cases, separate a direct quotation or maxim from the rest of the sentence by commas.

> "I am sorry," said the lawyer sadly, "that I can be of no help."

If the quote is restrictive appositive or used as the subject or predicate nominative, it should not be set off with commas.

> "When pigs fly" was a phrase Len least expected.

E. Semicolon (6.57–.62)

A semicolon marks a more important break in sentence flow than one marked by a comma.

1. Use a semicolon between two independent clauses not connected by a conjunction.

> Novels are steady moneymakers; particularly good sellers are apocalyptic stories.

2. The following adverbs should be preceded by a semicolon when used between clauses for a compound sentence:

then, however, thus, hence, indeed, accordingly, besides, and *therefore.* The exception to this rule involves clauses introduced by the adverbs *yet* and *so,* which are preceded by a comma.

> Lindsay forgot about volleyball practice; therefore, she did not play in the game.

> Joseph has made plans to finish graduate school, yet his course work is not complete.

3. Use a semicolon as an alternate way to separate a long compound sentence when either part of the sentence has a comma break.

> Silvia is an even-tempered, happy person, who always greets others with a smile; and she has a deep faith in God, remaining calm when difficulties arise.

4. You may choose to use semicolons for emphasis.

> It was the best of times; it was the worst of times.

5. Use semicolons to separate references (particularly Bible references) when they contain internal punctuation.

> Luke 1:1–4; 2:14, 21; 5:12, 14, 16.

6. Use semicolons for clarity to separate items in a long or complex series.

> The total number of those attending the conference was editors, 65; publishers, 30; writers, 47.

7. Always place semicolons outside quotation marks and parentheses.

> Luther once called the book of James "the epistle of straw"; however, he wrote a brilliant commentary on it.

F. Colon (6.63–.69)

A colon marks a discontinuity of grammatical construction greater than that indicated by a semicolon but less than a period. Its main function is to introduce material that follows immediately.

1. You may use a colon to emphasize a sequence in thought between two clauses that form a single sentence.

> Many in the congregation helped with the bake sale: twenty of them, for example, made pies.

2. A colon can also introduce a list or series.

> Nashville has at least three important tourist attractions: Broadway, Music Row, and LifeWay.

(If, however, the series is introduced by *namely, for instance, for example,* or *that is,* do not use a colon unless the series consists of one or more grammatically complete clauses: Nashville has at least three important tourist attractions, namely, Broadway, Music Row, and LifeWay.)

3. Use a colon between chapter and verse in Scripture passages.

> Matt. 2:5–13

G. Dash (6.80–.96)

1. Use an en dash (–) to indicate inclusive or continuing numbers, as in dates, page references or Scripture references.

> pp. 23–46
>
> 1861–65
>
> January–May 1994
>
> Acts 2:35–5:14

2. Use an em dash (—) to denote an abrupt break in thought that affects sentence structure.

> The emperor—he had been awake half the night waiting in vain for a reply—came down to breakfast in an angry mood.

3. Use a 2-em dash (no space on either side) to indicate missing letters in a word.

> Melody P——k voted no.

4. Use a 3-em dash (with space on each side) to indicate that a whole word has been omitted.

> The ship left ——— in May.

H. Quotation Marks (6.8–10, 11.1–.50)

1. Direct quotations must reproduce exactly the wording, spelling, and punctuation of the original, with one exception: It is acceptable to change the initial letter of the quotation to a capital or lowercase letter to fit the syntax of the text. Typographical errors that appear in modern works may be corrected, but idiosyncrasies of spelling in older works should be observed.

2. It is the author's responsibility to check every quotation against the original for accuracy.

3. Set quotations over eight lines in block quotes. You may insert shorter quotations within the text.

4. If the quotation, either run into or set off from the text, is used as part of the author's sentence, it begins with a lowercase letter, even though the original is a complete sentence and begins with a capital letter.

> The gospel of John begins with the assertion that "in the beginning was the Word."

5. Direct conversation, whether run into or set off from the text, should always be enclosed in quotation marks.

> Travis protested, "I simply do not like the taste of tofu in food!" He had just finished eating a small bowl of tofu chili. "Ugh! Tofu has no taste, in my opinion."

> "That's precisely why some people like it," Katie
> explained.

6. Quoted material set off from the text as a block quotation should not be enclosed in quotation marks. Quoted material within a block quotation should be enclosed in double quotation marks, even if the source used single quotation marks.

7. Scripture used in block quotations must be followed by the reference in parentheses. Another method is to put the reference on a separate line, with an em dash before and no parentheses.

8. The words *yes* and *no* should not be quoted except in direct discourse.

> Joshua always answered yes; he could not say no.

I. Parentheses (6.97–.103)

1. You may use parentheses, like commas and dashes, to set off amplifying, explanatory, or digressive elements. Use commas, however, if the two parts are closely related.

> He had long suspected that the inert gasses (helium,
> neon, argon, krypton) could be used to produce a
> similar effect.

2. You may enclose expressions such as *that is, namely, e.g., i.e.,* and the element introduced in parentheses if the break in thought is greater than that signaled by a comma.

> Bones from several animals (e.g., a dog, a cat, a
> squirrel, a pigeon) were found in the grave.

3. Use parentheses to enclose numerals or letters marking divisions or enumerations run into the text.

> The anthropologist stated there were no inexplicable

> differences between (1) Java man, (2) Neanderthal man, and, (3) Cro-Magnon man.

4. Place ending punctuation outside a closing parenthesis if the word or phrase in the parentheses interrupts or is interjected into a sentence. When a question mark or an exclamation point is part of the parenthetical matter, place the question mark or exclamation point inside the closing parenthesis.

> A consistent format should be followed (do not punctuate by ear).

> A consistent format should be followed (never punctuate by ear!).

5. You can follow ending punctuation of a sentence by separate parenthetical matter that is also a sentence or complete thought. The parenthetical matter may be related to but independent of the previous sentence.

> Was this a desperate cry for help? (Or any one of a hundred other considerations?)

6. When quoting Scripture, place the period after the parentheses containing the reference. If the quotation requires a question mark or exclamation point, place it with the text, and place the period after the last parenthesis. When quoting Scripture that is set off from the text as a block quotation, place the period after the Scripture text.

> "In the beginning God created the heaven and the earth" (Gen. 1:1).

> "Lord, are You going to wash my feet?" (John 13:6).

J. Brackets (6.104–.110)

1. Brackets enclose editorial interpolations, corrections, explanations, or comments.

> Jesus told Nicodemus, "Unless someone is born again [born anew, or born from above] he cannot see the Kingdom of God."

> He [Robert E. Lee] died in 1870, never having received a pardon from the United States government.

2. Brackets may also enclose the phonetic transcript of a word.

> He attributed the light to the phenomenon called *gegenschein* [ga-gen-shin].

K. Ellipses (11.51–.71)

1. Indicate any omission of a word, phrase, line, or paragraph from a quoted passage by ellipsis points, with a space before and after each dot.

2. Three dots . . . indicate that material is deleted at the beginning or within a sentence.

> "By faith Moses . . . was hidden by his parents . . . because they saw that the child was beautiful" (Heb. 11:23).

3. You may use other punctuation on either side of the three ellipsis dots if it makes the meaning clearer.

> I wondered, was he the hapless dupe he made out to be? . . . He seemed far too clever for that.

4. Three dots . . . may also indicate a break in thought, daydreaming, or hesitation. Use an en dash, however, to indicate an *external* interruption of speech or thought.

> If he had only come sooner . . . if only . . . then perhaps everything would have been different. I—that is, we—yes, we wish he had come sooner.

5. Unless the content requires such, it is not usually necessary to use ellipsis points before or after a verse or a

portion of a Scripture verse. Introductory words such as *and* and *for* may be omitted from a Scripture quotation without using ellipsis points.

> "For God loved the world in this way . . ." (John 3:16)
> may correctly read "God loved the world in this
> way . . ."

6. Four dots . . . . indicate that material is omitted at the end of a sentence (the extra dot accounts for the period). The missing material could be (1) the last part of a quoted sentence, (2) the first part of the next sentence, (3) a whole sentence or more, (4) a whole paragraph or more.

> "Now all the believers were together and had every-
> thing in common. . . . Every day they devoted them-
> selves to meeting together" (Acts 2:44, 46).

7. If the original quotation is punctuated with a question mark or an exclamation point, retain this mark and use three dots for the ellipsis.

> "Now is my soul troubled. What should I say—'Father,
> save me from this hour?' . . . Father, glorify your
> name!" (John 12:27).

L. Apostrophe (7.17–.32)

1. The apostrophe is the mark of the possessive. The possessive case of singular nouns is formed by the addition of an apostrophe and an *s*, and the possessive of plural nouns by the addition of an apostrophe only.

> the book's cover
>
> the puppies' tails

2. When you can do it without confusion, form the plural of numbers and letters used as words by adding *s* alone.

the three Rs
four YMCAs
the early 1930s

3. Abbreviations with periods, lowercase letters used as nouns, and some capital letters may require an apostrophe for clarity, even when not used in a possessive sense.

M.Div.'s   xs and ys
Th.D.'s   S's, A's, I's

4. The general rule for forming the possessive of common nouns (apostrophe and an s for singular names, an s followed by an apostrophe for plural names—see number 1 above) also applies to proper names, including most names of any length ending in sibilants.

Susie's swimming pool

Steve's messy office

Rosses' house (but Ross's house, when the word refers to just one person)

Burns's poems

Exceptions: The names Jesus and Moses are traditional exceptions to the general rule for forming the possessive.

Jesus' disciples

Moses' staff

M. Solidus/Slash/Slant/Virgule (6.111–.119)

1. Related to the dash and the hyphen in form and function, the solidus (/) sometimes indicates alternatives and alternative word forms or spellings and replaces *and* in some sentences.

> Qur'an/Koran
>
> Sales figures rose dramatically in the June/July period.
>
> Miss Holley's bridal bouquet will feature daisies and/or primroses.

2. A solidus with no spaces before or after can indicate that a time period spans two consecutive years, though the en dash is preferable.

> Winter 1910/11 or Winter 1910–11 (preferable)

3. When poetry or text from songs is run into the text, a solidus with a space both before and after it designates line breaks.

> As Thomas Gray once observed, "Full many a flower was born to blush unseen / And waste its sweetness on the desert air."

N. Diacritical Marks and Special Characters (10.14)

English is one of very few languages that can be set without accents, diacritics, or special alphabetic characters for native words. Editors and typesetters may recognize the more common marks used in foreign words such as ¿, á, è, or ñ, but may not be familiar with ones used in other languages (i.e., classical Greek, Hebrew, or Chinese). Authors need to mark their manuscripts clearly when they use such a mark or notify the editor if there will be a need to use a special typeface.

CHAPTER 3
Elements of Style

A. Italics (7.49–.81)

1. The use of italics can emphasize a word or phrase.

> But the *actual* cause of the accident is yet to be determined.

2. It is often helpful to set a technical term, especially when it is accompanied by its definition, in italics the first time it appears in the text.

> *Tabular matter* is copy, usually consisting of figures, which is set in columns.

3. Italicize isolated words or phrases in a foreign language if they are unfamiliar to most readers.

> *Caveat Emptor!*
>
> *Ein feste Burg ist unser Gott*
>
> *sine qua non*

Exception: You do not need to italicize foreign expressions used so commonly that they have become a recognized part of the English language.

per se	ad hoc	quid pro quo	Wiener schnitzel
ad lib	hacienda	habeas corpus	coup de grace

4. To clarify a person's thoughts in contrast to one's verbal discourse, italics is a good choice.

> I looked over the unarmed bushwhacker who was attempting to rob me. *He can't be serious,* I thought to myself.

5. Italicize references to words as words.

> The word *faith* has often been confused with hope.

6. Use italics for book titles, movies, ships, and for radio or TV programs in continuing series. Set titles of individual programs not in continuing series in Roman type and quotation marks.

> *Screwtape Letters*
>
> USS *Yorktown*
>
> *Gunsmoke*
>
> NBC's series, *West Wing*
>
> "Beverly Sills Sings at the Met"

B. Hyphenation (7.81–.90)

1. Use hyphens cautiously. Most compound words do not require a hyphen. Most noun combinations that were formerly hyphenated are now written as solid words: butterfat, willpower. Others are still hyphenated: well-being. Some that were once hyphenated are now two words: water supply. Keep a copy of *Merriam-Webster's Collegiate Dictionary, Eleventh Edition* on hand so as not to hyphenate by intuition.

2. A word or phrase used as an adjective is often hyphenated, but it may not be hyphenated when used as a noun.

soul-winning program
Soul winning (noun) was her mission.

3. Dividing a word for typographical purposes is tricky. If not sure where to divide, consult the *Merriam Webster's Collegiate Dictionary, Eleventh Edition,* and/or *Chicago Manual of Style, Fifteenth Edition,* Sections 7.33–.45.

C. Abbreviations (15.1–.76)

1. Do not use abbreviations for given names (unless the person himself wrote his name in that fashion).

William not Wm.

Charles not Chas.

2. When you use a civil or military title with the surname alone, spell out the individual's title.

General Eisenhower

Lieutenant Jenkins

If you use the person's full name and title, however, you may abbreviate the title.

Sen. Bill Frist

Col. Jack Papworth Goss

3. Always use the standard abbreviations for Mr., Mrs., Ms., and Dr.

4. Add the article *the* to the title *Reverend.* When you abbreviate the title, you may drop the article, but it should be accompanied by a full name (except in fiction).

the Reverend Billy Sunday

the Reverend Mr. Sunday

Rev. Billy Sunday

5. It is proper style to abbreviate the names of government agencies, organizations, associations, some corporations,

and other groups. In most cases, set these abbreviations in capitals without periods.

NATO	ASPCA	ABC Network
ECPA	CBA	WPLN, Nashville Public Radio
AAR/SBL	SBC	NAPCE

The same applies to famous persons known by their initials only.

FDR	RFK

6. Always spell out the names of states, territories, and possessions of the United States when they stand alone in text.

> The state of Arizona
>
> Charlie moved to Nashville, Tennessee, to try his luck in the country music business.

7. Spell out the names of countries in the text. (*United States* is preferred over *U.S.* (United States used as an adjective may be abbreviated to U.S. in informal writing, i.e., U.S. currency.)

8. Spell out names of the months in the text, whether alone or in dates. It is acceptable form to abbreviate them in chronologies or footnotes.

Jan.	July
Feb.	Aug.
Mar.	Sept.
Apr.	Oct.
May	Nov.
June	Dec.

9. Always spell out the names of the days of the week.

10. It is standard style to abbreviate parts of a book in footnotes or bibliographies, but do not abbreviate them in the text.

appendix	app.
book	bk.
figure	fig.
folio	fol.
notes(s)	n. (plural is nn.)
number	no.
page(s)	p. (plural is pp.)
paragraph	par.
volume	vol. (plural is vols.)

D. Abbreviations and Scripture References (15.47–.54)

1. In text, spell out references to whole books or whole chapters of the Bible.

> The opening chapters of Ephesians . . .

> Genesis records the creation of the world in the first two chapters.

2. You may abbreviate biblical references when you enclose them in parentheses. In some scholarly or reference works and under some conditions, you may abbreviate them in the text. (See "Academic Requirements" in chapter 7 for correct Bible book abbreviation forms for academic works.)

Old Testament

Gen.	1 Sam.	Esther
Exod.	2 Sam.	Job
Lev.	1 Kings	Ps.
Num.	2 Kings	Prov.
Deut.	1 Chron.	Eccles.
Josh.	2 Chron.	Song of Sol.
Judg.	Ezra	Isa.
Ruth	Neh.	Jer.

Lam.	Amos	Hab.
Ezek.	Obad.	Zeph.
Dan.	Jonah	Hag.
Hosea	Mic.	Zech.
Joel	Nah.	Mal.

New Testament

Matt.	Eph.	Heb.
Mark	Phil.	James
Luke	Col.	1 Pet.
John	1 Thess.	2 Pet.
Acts	2 Thess.	1 John
Rom.	1 Tim.	2 John
1 Cor.	2 Tim.	3 John
2 Cor.	Titus	Jude
Gal.	Philem.	Rev.

Refer to books of the Bible with the title used in the version you cite. For example, the full name for Song of Solomon is "Song of Songs" in the *New International Version* and is not abbreviated.

3. Use Arabic numerals for all references. If the reference begins a sentence, however, spell out the number.

. . . in 1 John . . .

First John 3:16 says . . .

E. Abbreviations of Scripture Versions

It is standard practice to abbreviate versions of Scripture in references.

Amplified	*The Amplified Bible*
ASV	*American Standard Version*
AV	*Authorized (King James) Version*
CEV	*Contemporary English Version*
ESV	*English Standard Version*

GW	*God's Word: Today's Bible Translation*
JB	*Jerusalem Bible*
HCSB	*Holman Christian Standard Bible*
KJV	*King James Version* (also known as *Authorized Version*)
Lamsa	*The Holy Bible from Ancient Eastern Manuscripts*
LB	*Living Bible*
MLB	*Modern Language Bible/New Berkeley*
Moffatt	*A New Translation of the Bible*
NASB	*New American Standard Bible*
NASBU	*New American Standard Bible Update*
NCV	*New Century Version*
NEB	*New English Bible*
NET	*New Evangelical Translation*
NIV	*New International Version*
NJB	*New Jerusalem Bible*
NKJV	*New King James Version*
NLT	*New Living Translation*
NRSV	*New Revised Standard Version*
Phillips	*The New Testament in Modern English*
RNASB	*Revised New American Standard Bible*
RSV	*Revised Standard Version*
RV	*Revised Version*
SEB	*The Simple English Bible*
TEV	*Today's English Version*
TNIV	*Today's New International Version*

5. The abbreviation for verse is v. and for verses, vv.

v. 23

vv. 24–26

CHAPTER 4
Use of Numbers in Text

A. General Rules (9.1–.71)

1. Write exact numbers under 100 as words and numbers 100 or larger in numerals.

> Our ten editors work tirelessly twenty-four hours a day.
>
> Joseph has at least 525 vintage baseball cards.
>
> The junior choir consisted of sixty children.

2. Spell out round numbers in hundreds, thousands, or millions, but list exact numbers larger than one hundred in numerals.

> four billion
>
> 3.6 billion
>
> 2,486
>
> 237

3. Two exceptions to this rule are year numbers and numbers referring to parts of the book.

> 44 BC   page 7
>
> AD 1999

4. Spell out initial numbers at the beginning of a sentence.

> One hundred forty years ago . . .
>
> Twenty-five percent . . .

5. Use commas between every group of three digits in figures of one thousand or more.

> 56,925
>
> 2,414

Exceptions to this rule are page numbers, addresses, and year numbers of four digits, which are written in figures without commas.

> He found the definition for *truffle* on page 1268.

6. In statistical, technical, or scientific copy, it is acceptable to write numbers that precede units of measurement as numerals, as well as to abbreviate the units. You may also use the ° symbol (the typographical symbol for *degrees*) for temperature measurement.

> 3 cubic inches
>
> 76 pounds
>
> 11 lb.
>
> 22 ft.
>
> 6 gal.
>
> 60 volts
>
> 32° F.
>
> 9 hrs.

7. In scientific and technical copy, use the symbol "%" for a percentage; in other copy, use the word *percent*.

> Of the citizens polled, more than 82% are in favor of the referendum.
>
> The loan has an interest rate of 7 percent.

In statistical or technical discussions, use numerals for percentages.

> The author claims that only 10 percent of evangelicals define themselves as doctrinal people.

8. Spell out percentages when they begin a sentence and when you use them in a literary or informal way.

> Ninety-nine percent of all editors think they are woefully underpaid.

> I imagine that ninety-seven percent of editors are bookworms.

9. Set decimal fractions, including academic grades, in figures, both in literary and scientific copy.

> A grade point average of 3.9 is considered outstanding.

10. Numbers applicable to the same category should be consistent throughout a paragraph. If the largest number contains three or more digits, use figures for all.

11. Where you use two adjacent numbers, spell out one of them for the sake of clarity.

> sixty 12-inch rulers   200 ten-cent stamps

12. Use a period without parentheses after numbers in a vertical listing.

> 1.
>
> 2.
>
> 3.

13. Enclose numerals in a list within a paragraph in double parentheses, or use an end parenthesis after a numeral. Do not follow the numeral with a period in either case.

> There were three areas of concern for the new product division: (1) production, (2) marketing, and (3) distribution.

There were three areas of concern for the new product division: 1) production, 2) . . .

B. Currency (9.23–.29)

1. Follow general rules for numbers in regard to isolated references to money in United States currency, and either spell them or represent them in figures as the rules specify.

> I'll give five dollars for the fund.
>
> Each employee received $42.20 for wages, $11.44 for benefits, and $2.40 for cost of living.

2. Substitute the words *million* and *billion* for zeros, but spell out round numbers in thousands.

> $6 million   ten thousand dollars

C. Dates and Times (9.33-.45)

1. Spell out in lowercase letters your references to particular centuries and decades.

> nineteenth century
>
> sixties and seventies (Exception: 1940s)

2. Write dates consistently in one of the following forms. Never use *st, nd, rd,* or *th* after figures in dates.

> October 14, 1964
>
> *Saturday Review,* 12 October 1968, 32
>
> The third of June 1943
>
> June 9 (never June 9th)

3. You should usually spell out times of day in the text.

> The church meeting wasn't over until four-thirty.

However, you may use figures to emphasize the exact time.

The train arrived at 3:22.

4. Use numeric figures and regular capital letters in designations of time with AM or PM. Lowercase with periods is also accepable.

2:00 PM   8:25 a.m.

D. Street Names and Addresses (9.55–.57)

In most cases, represent house or highway numbers or street addresses in figures.

6556 North Glenwood

121 Beale Street

Interstate 57

Exceptions: Fifth Avenue, Forty-second Street, One LifeWay Plaza

CHAPTER 5
Capitalization (8.1–.210)

A. Titles of Offices (8.21–.35)

1. Capitalize civil, military, religious, and professional titles when they immediately precede a personal name.

> President McKinley
>
> General Patton
>
> Reverend C. A. Pagel
>
> Chief Engineer Barry Dean
>
> Cardinal Newman

2. In text matter, titles following a personal name or used alone in place of a name should be lowercase, with rare exceptions.

> Abraham Lincoln, president of the United States
>
> President Lincoln, the president of the United States
>
> the president; presidential; presidency
>
> General Ulysses S. Grant, commander in chief of the Union army
>
> General Grant
>
> the commander in chief

the general

George VI, king of England

the king of England; the king

the bishop of London

Edward J. Goss, counsel for the defense

Kari Drost, M.D.

3. Capitalize titles that you use in place of names in direct address.

I'm sorry, Officer, the accelerator stuck.

B. Kinship Names (8.39)

Put a kinship name in lowercase when it is not followed by a given name, but capitalize it in direct address or when you substitute the term for a personal name.

his father

my brothers and sister

Uncle Phil

Aunt Sara

Rosenberg is my mother's maiden name.

Ask Sister to give you a bite of hers.

Don't go near the water, Son.

Did you sell your house yet, Auntie?

Cheryl and Cindy are his youngest aunts.

C. Political Divisions (8.55–.56)

In general, capitalize words designating political divisions of the world, a country, state, city, and similar entities when they follow the name or when they are an accepted or official part of the name.

Roman Empire; but the empire under Diocletian; the
empire

Washington State; the state of Washington

D. Organizations (8.66–.76)

1. Capitalize names of national and international
organizations, movements and alliances, and members of
political parties, but do not capitalize the words *movement, platform,* and similar terms.

Republican Party; Republican platform; Republicans(s)

Common Market

Loyalist(s)

Now is the time for all good men and women to come
to the aid of their party.

2. Represent nouns and adjectives designating political
and economic systems of thought and their proponents in
lowercase, unless the term is used in a restricted, official
way.

bolshevism

communism

democracy

democrat (a general advocate of democracy); democratic
principles

republican (a general advocate of republicanism)

Marxism

E. Words Derived from Geographical Locations or Proper Names (8.46–.54, 8.64–.65)

Put words that have their root in geographical locations or proper names into lowercase when you choose them for their specialized meaning. (There are some exceptions, such as *Spanish moss;* if in doubt, check *Merriam Webster's Collegiate Dictionary, Eleventh Edition* or *Chicago Manual of Style, Fifteenth Edition.*)

dutch oven	india ink
french fries	diesel fuel

F. Holidays/Seasons (8.94–.96)

1. Lowercase the four seasons unless you personify them.

> We welcomed the arrival of spring.
>
> Then Winter—with her icy blasts—subsided.

2. Capitalize the names of religious holidays and seasons.

> Christmas Eve
>
> Easter, or Easter Sunday
>
> Pentecost
>
> Passover

3. Capitalize secular holidays and other specially designated days.

> Fourth of July; the Fourth
>
> Mother's Day
>
> Thanksgiving Day

G. Religious Terms (8.97–.119)

1. Capitalize the names of the one supreme God.

God

Abba

Adonai

(the) Father

Logos

Jehovah

(the) Word

(the) Redeemer

Yahweh

(the) Savior

Master

(the) Son

Holy Spirit

Christ

2. Some Christian publishers differ from *The Chicago Manual of Style* in that they often capitalize pronouns referring to God in their books for the general reading audience. Check with your publisher regarding their preference and make consistent use of their rules. (Exceptions: Do not capitalize *who* or *whom*.)

Trust in Him.

God gives man what He wants.

Jesus and His disciples

Jesus knew He was the one who must die on the cross.

3. Though the names of specific places in Scripture are normally capitalized, put *heaven, hell,* and *hades* in lowercase.

4. Capitalize adjectives derived from proper names—e.g., Mosaic dispensation; Christian era; Maccabean period; Messianic age.

5. The following list of biblical and religious terms are capitalized or lowercased according to preferred style at most Christian publishers:

Abba
abomination of desolation, the
Abraham's Bosom
Abrahamic covenant
absolution
abyss, the
AD (AD 70 but 400 BC)
Adonai
adoptionism
Advent
Adventist(s)
adversary, the (Satan)
Advocate (Christ)
agape (Greek word for *love*)
agnosticism
Agnus Dei (Latin for *Lamb of God*)
AH (Anno Hebraica, in the Hebrew Year)
Albigensians
All Saints' Day (or All Hallows Eve)
All Souls' Day
Allah
alleluia
Almighty God

Almighty, the
Alpha and Omega (Christ)
altar
amillenarian
amillennialism
amillennialist
Amish
Anabaptist(s)
Ancient of Days, the (God)
angel
angel Gabriel, the
angel Jibril (Islamic version of Gabriel)
angel of the Lord
Angel of the Lord (if used as a theophany)
Anglo-Catholicism
Anglo-Saxon Church
Anima Christi (Latin for *Soul of Christ*)
annihilationism
Anno Domini
annunciation, the
Anointed One, the (Jesus Christ)
Anointed, the
anointing of the sick

ante-Christian

Ante Christum (BC; Latin for *Before Christ*)

ante-Nicene fathers

antiabortion, antiabortionist

antibiblical

Antichrist, the

anti-Christian

antinomian(s)

anti-Semitic, anti-Semite, anti-Semitism

anti-Trinitarian

Aphrodite

Apocalypse, the (Revelation)

apocalyptic literature

Apocrypha, the

apocryphal (adjective)

Apollonarianism

Apollonian

apologetics

apostasy, apostasies

apostate, apostatize

apostle

apostle Peter, Peter the apostle

Apostle to the Gentiles (Paul)

apostles

Apostles' Creed

apostolic age

apostolic benediction

apostolic council

apostolic faith

apostolic succession

Aramaic

archangel

archdeacon, archdeaconry

archdiocese

archenemy

archrival

Arian, Arianism

ark, the (Noah's)

ark narratives, the

ark of testimony

ark of the covenant

Armageddon

Arminian, Arminianism

Articles of Religion, the (Methodism)

AS (Anno Salutis, in the year of salvation)

Ascension Day

ascension of Christ, the

Ascension, the

ascetic, asceticism

Ash Wednesday

Ashkenazi Jew

Association of Research and Enlightenment (movement, also known as A.R.E.)

Assyrian Empire, the

astrology

Athanasian Creed

atheism

Atonement, the

atonement of Christ, the

Augsburg Confession

Authorized Version (or King James Version)

avatar

ayatollah (but Ayatollah Khomeni)

B'nai B'rith
Baals of Canaan
babe (of Bethlehem)
baby Jesus, the
Babylonian captivity
Babylonian exile
Baha'i (movement), Bahaism, Bahaist
Balaam
banshee
baptism, baptismal, baptize
baptism of the Holy Spirit
Baptism, the (of Christ); but Christ's baptism
baptistery (or baptistry)
baptistic
bar mitzvah
barbarian
Barmen Declaration
Basel, Confession of
bat (or bas or bath) mitzvah
Battle of Armageddon
BC (400 BC, but AD 70)
BCE (Before the Common Era)
Beast, the (Antichrist)
Beatific Vision
Beatitudes, the (Sermon on the Mount)
Beelzebub
Beghards
Being (God)
believers church
Beloved Apostle, the
Benedictines
benediction

beneficence
benison
Bereans
Beth Shan
betrayal, the (of Christ)
Bhagavad Gita (or Bhagavadgita)
Bible Belt
Bible school
Bible, the
Bible conference (but Niagara Bible Conference)
biblical
blasphemy
blessed name (Christ)
Blessing of Jacob
blood of Christ
bodhisattva (or boddhisattva)
body of Christ (the church)
book of Genesis, the (et al.)
Book of Life
book of the annals of Solomon, the
book of the annals of the kings of Israel (Judah et al.), the
Book of the Covenant
Book of the Dead
Book of the Law
Book of the Twelve, the
Book of Truth
Book, the (Bible)
born-again (adjective)
boy Jesus, the
brazen altar
Bread of Life (Bible or Christ)

Breeches Bible
bride of Christ (the church)
bridegroom, the (Christ)
brotherhood of man
Buddha, Buddhism, Buddhist
burnt offering
Byzantine
Cabala, Cabbalah (or Kabala)
Calvary
Calvinism
Canaan, Canaanite(s)
Canon, the (Scripture)
canon law
canon of Scripture, the
canonical
Captivity, the
catholic (universal)
Catholic Church (Roman
    Catholic)
Catholic Epistles (James et al.)
Catholicism
cause (of Christ)
CE (Common Era)
celestial city
century, first, nineteenth et al.
Chalcedon, Council of
Chanukah or Hanukkah (Feast of
    the Dedication)
charisma
charismatic
charismatic Christian
charismatic church
charismatic movement, the
charismatics
cherub, cherubim

chief priest
Chief Shepherd (Christ)
child of God (Christian)
Children of God, the (movement,
    also known as the Family of
    Love)
children of Israel
chosen people, the (Jews)
Christ
Christ child
Christ event
Christadelphians, the
christen, christened, christening
Christendom
Christian
Christian Brothers
Christian era
Christian Reformed Church
Christian Science (movement)
Christianize, Christianization
Christianlike
Christlike
Christmas Day
Christmas Eve
Christmastide
Christological
Christology
Christus Victor
Chronicler, the
church (body of Christ, universal)
church (building, service, local)
church age
church and state
church fathers
church invisible

church militant
Church of England
Church of Rome
church-planting (adj.)
church triumphant
church universal
church visible
church year, the (calendar)
City of David
City of the Lord (Jerusalem)
Cloud of Unknowing (classic
    mystical book)
codex (but Codex Sinaiticus)
collect (written prayer)
Comforter, the (Holy Spirit)
commandment (first, tenth,
    et al.)
commandment (generic term)
(Ten) Commandments, the
Communion (Lord's Supper)
Communion of Saints
Communion service
Complutensian Polyglot Bible
Concord, Book of
Concord, Formula of
Confessing Church
confession
Confession of Augsburg
confirmation
Confucian, Confucianism,
    Confucianist
Confucius
Congregationalists
consecration
Conservative Baptist

conservative, conservatism
consubstantiation
Corpus Christi (Latin for *body of
    Christ*)
Council of Nicea, Council of
    Trent, etc.
Counselor, the
covenant of grace
covenant of works
covenant theologian
Covenant Theology
covenant, the
covet
Creation, the
creation of man, the
Creationism
Creator, the
creed (but Nicene Creed, etc.)
cross (the object)
cross, the (event, not object)
Crucifixion, the
crucifixion of Christ
Crusades, the
cryptogram
cult
curate
curse, the
Daniel's Seventieth Week
Davidic covenant
Davidic dynasty
Davidic law
David's court
Day (capitalize when part of
    name of holiday or day
    marked by special observance)

Day of Atonement (Yom Kippur)
day of grace
Day of Judgment
Day of Pentecost
Day of the Lord
deacon (but Deacon Smith)
Dead Sea Scrolls
Decalogue, the
decree of Cyrus
deism, deist(s)
deity of Christ
Deity, the (God)
deluge, the (the flood)
Demiurge (God)
demon, demonic, demonolatry, demonology
determinism
deus ex machina
Deuteronomic
devil
Devil, the (Satan)
dharma
Diaspora, the (dispersion of Israel)
Didache
disciple(s)
Disciples of Christ
Dispensation of the Law
dispensationalism, dispensationalist
Dispersion, the
Dissenters (specific religious movement)
divine
Divine Father

divine guidance
divine judgment
Divine Providence
divinity of Christ, the
Divinity, the (God)
Docetism
Doctors of the Church (title for Ambrose, Augustine of Hippo, Gregory the Great, and Jerome)
doctrinal, doctrine
Documentary Hypothesis
dogma, dogmatic
Donatism
Door, the (Christ)
Douay (Rheims-Douay) Version
double predestination
Downgrade Controversy
doxology (but Gloria Patri)
Dragon, the (Satan)
dualism
early church
earth (dirt or ground, or when meaning *world*)
Earth (planet)
Easter morning
Easter Sunday
Eastern church
Eastern Orthodox Church
Eastern religions
Eastern rites
Ebionitism
ecclesia (or ekklesia)
ecclesiology
Eckankar (movement)

ecumenical movement
ecumenism, ecumenical
efficacious grace
Egnatian Way (Via Egnatia)
El
El Shaddai
election
Eleven, the
Elohim
Emmaus road
end times, the
Enemy, the (Satan)
England, Church of
Enlightenment, the
Epiphany
episcopacy, episcopal (relating to
    church government)
Episcopalian (denomination)
epistemological, epistemology
epistle (John's epistle et al.)
Epistle to the Romans et al.
Epistles, the (apostolic letters)
eschatology, eschatological
eschaton, the
Essene(s)
est (movement, stands for
    Erhard Seminars Training)
Eternal, the (God)
Eternal God
eternal life
eternity
Eucharist, the
Evangel, the
evangelical (adj., but First
    Evangelical Sunday School)

evangelical(s) (noun)
Evangelicalism (the movement)
Evangelist (Gospel writer)
evangelist (one who evangelizes)
Evil One, the (Satan)
ex cathedra
ex officio
Executor of justice, the (God)
exegesis
Exile, the
exodus from Egypt, the
Exodus, the
exorcism
expiation
extrabiblical
extreme unction
faith, the (Christian)
faith healing
fakir
Fall, the
fall of man
False Prophet (of Revelation)
Family of Love, the (movement,
    also known as the Children
    of God)
Father (God)
Father of Lies (Satan)
fatherhood of God
Fathers, the (but church fathers)
fatweh
feast
Feast of the Passover (Booths,
    Dedication, Esther, Firstfruits,
    Lights, Purim, Tabernacles,
    Unleavened Bread)

first Adam
First Advent, the
First Vatican Council, etc.
Firstborn, the (Christ)
Five Pillars of Faith (Islam)
Five Points of Calvinism
Flood, the
Formal Cause
four gospels, the (but the
    Gospels, when using as a title)
Four Kingdoms, the
Foursquare Gospel, International
    Church of the
Franciscans
free will (n), freewill (adj.)
Free Will Baptist
Freemason(s), Freemasonry
Friend (when meaning God,
    Christ, or the Holy Spirit)
fundamentalists (but
    Fundamentalism when refer-
    ring to the movement)
fundamentals of the faith
futurist(s)
Galilean, the (Christ)
Galilee, Sea of (but Galilean sea)
Garden of Eden
garden, the
gatekeeper
gehenna
General Epistles
gentile (adj.)
Gentile(s)
Geschichte (German for history)
Gethsemane, Garden of

Gezer
Gloria Patri (but the doxology)
glory cloud
glossolalia
gnostic (generic or descriptive)
Gnosticism (specific form of)
God
god (pagan)
God of gods and Lord of lords
God's house
God's Word (Bible)
God's word (promise)
Godhead (essential being of God)
godhead (godship or godhood)
godless
godlike
godly
God-man
godsend
Godspeed
Golden Rule, the
golden text
Golgotha
Good Book, the
Good Friday
Good News, the (i.e., the Gospel)
Good Samaritan, the
Good Shepherd (Jesus)
good shepherd, the parable of the
gospel (adj.)
gospel (John's gospel et al.)
gospel, the (specific New
    Testament concept of the
    good news or God's
    redemption)

Gospel(s), the
grace
Great Awakening
Great Commandment
Great Commission
Great High Priest (Christ)
Great Judgment
Great King
Great Physician
Great Schism
Great Shepherd
Great Tribulation
Great White Throne
Grecian
Greek
Guide, the (Holy Spirit)
hades (hell)
Hades (mythological)
Hagiographa
hagiographer, hagiographic,
    hagiography
Hail Mary
Hallel
hallelujah
Hannah's song
Hanukkah or Chanukah (Feast of
    the Dedication)
Hare Krishnas, the (movement,
    also known as the
    International Society of
    Krishna Consciousness)
Head, the (Christ, head of the
    church)
heaven
heavenly Father

Hebraic
Hebrew
Hebrew Bible
Hebrew patriarchs
Hegira (Muhammad's)
Heidelberg Catechism
Heilsgeschichte (German for
    salvation history)
hell
Hellenism, Hellenistic
Helvetic Confessions
hermeneutics
Herod's temple
Herodian
heterodoxy
High Church (Anglican)
high priest, a
High Priest, the (Christ)
High Priestly Prayer, the (Christ's)
higher criticism
Hillel
Historical Books, the (part of the
    Old Testament)
historical-grammatical
    hermeneutics
historicist(s)
Holiness Movement, the
holocaust (when referring to a
    general destruction or sacri-
    fice or fire, etc.)
Holocaust (when referring to the
    specific event during World
    War II)
Holy Bible
Holy Book (Bible)

Holy City (Jerusalem)
Holy Club, the (Oxford)
Holy Communion
Holy Eucharist
holy family
Holy Ghost
Holy Grail
Holy Land (Palestine)
Holy of Holies
holy oil
Holy One, the (God, Christ)
Holy One of Israel, the (God)
holy orders
holy place
Holy Roller
Holy Saturday
Holy Scriptures
Holy Spirit
Holy Thursday
Holy Trinity
holy water
Holy Week (before Easter)
Holy Writ (Bible)
Holy Year (Catholic)
homeland
homiletics, homilies, homily
house of David
house of the Lord
Huguenots
Humanae Vitae (Latin for *human lives*)
Hussites
Hutterites
hymnal
hymnbook

hypostatic union
ichthus
icon
idealist(s)
idolatry
illuminati
imago dei (Latin for *image of God*)
Immaculate Conception, the
Immanuel
immortality of the soul
in excelsis
incarnation of Christ, the
Incarnation, the
inerrancy, inerrant
infallibility
inner veil
Inquisition, the
inspiration
intercession
Intercessor, the (Christ)
intertestamental
intifada
invisible church
Isaian (or Isaianic)
Islamic Jihad (the organization, but jihad, in a general sense)
Jacob's Trouble
Jacobites
Jebusites
Jehovah
Jehovah's Witnesses (officially, the Watchtower Bible and Tract Society)

Jeremian (or Jeremianic)
Jerome
Jerusalem
Jesuits (Society of Jesus, but jesuitical)
Jesus Christ
Jesus Prayer, the
Jew(s)
Jewish (adj.)
Jewish Feast (Passover)
Jewish New Year (Rosh Hashanah/Hoshanah)
Jewish Talmud
Jew's (Jews') harp
jihad (but Islamic Jihad, when referring to a specific organization)
Johannine
John the Baptist
John the Evangelist
Jordan River (but the river Jordan)
Jordan Valley
Josephus
Jubilee (year of emancipation)
Judah, Judahite
Judaic, Judaica
Judaism, Judaist, Judaistic
Judaize(r)
Judea
Judean
Judeo-Christian
Judge (the Lord)
judges, the
Judgment Day

judgment seat of Christ, the
Judgment, Great White Throne
Judgment, the Last
justification
Kaddish (special prayer)
kenosis, kenosistic
kerygma
Keswick Convention
kibbutz, kibbutzim
king
King (God or Jesus)
King David, King Herod, etc.
King James Version
King of Glory (Christ)
King of kings
King of kings (God the only Ruler)
King of the Jews
Kingdom, the (God's)
kingdom age
kingdom of God
kingdom of heaven
kingdom of Israel
kingdom of Satan
Kings (books of 1 and 2 Kings as single literary work)
kingship of Christ
Kinsman-Redeemer
Knesset (Israel's governing body)
koine
koinonia
Koran (but prefer Qur'an)
koranic
Lady Folly
Lady Wisdom

laity
lake of fire
Lamb, the (Christ)
Lamb of God
Lamb's Book of Life
land of Canaan
land of Goshen
Land of Promise
Last Day, the
last days, the
Last Judgment, the
last rites (extreme unction)
Last Supper, the
Late Bronze Age (1550–1200 BC)
Latin Rite
Latin Vulgate
Latter Rain movement
law (as opposed to grace)
Law, the (Pentetuch)
law and the prophets, the
law of Moses, a (general)
Law of Moses, the
Lawgiver (God)
layperson
Lent, Lenten
Leviathan
Levites, Levitical
liberal, liberalism
Liberation Theology
Light (Christ)
limbo (Roman Catholic
    theological term)
Litany, the (Anglican), but litany
    in a general sense

liturgy
living God
living Word, the (Bible)
Logos, the (Jesus)
Lord of hope (of love, of faith-
    fulness, of salvation, etc.)
Lord of Hosts
Lord of Lords
Lord, the
Lord's Anointed, the (Christ)
Lord's Day, the
Lord's Prayer, the (or the Our
    Father)
Lord's Supper, the
Lord's Table, the
lordship of Christ, the
Lost Tribes, the (BUT lost tribes
    of Israel)
Love Chapter, the
Low Church (Anglican)
Lucan (or Lukan)
Lucifer
Luther's Ninety-five Theses
Lutheran, Lutheranism
Maccabees
Magi
Magisterium
Magnificat, the
Mahabharata
major prophets (people)
Major Prophets, the (Old
    Testament)
Majority Text
Maker (God)

mammon
Man of Sin
Man of Sorrows
Maranatha
Marcan (or Markan)
Marcionism
martyrdom
Masoretic text
mass (service)
Mass, the (sacrament)
Master (the one supreme God)
Master, the (Christ)
Matthean
matzo ball
Maundy Thursday (Holy Thursday)
mazel tov
Mediator, the (Christ)
medieval
Mediterranean
megachurch
Megiddo
Mennonites
menorah
mercy seat
Mesopotamia, Mesopotamian
Messiah, the (Christ)
messianic
Messianic King
Methodist, Methodism
Middle East, Middle Eastern
midrash
midtribulation, midtribulational, midtribulationism, midtribulationist

millenarian, millenarianism, millenarianist
millennial kingdom (note the -*ll* and -*nn* spellings)
millennialist, millennialism
millennium, millenniums, millennia (1,000 years)
Millennium, the
mini-narratives
minor prophets (people)
Minor Prophets (the books)
Miserere, the
Mishnah
misseo Dei
Moabite Stone, the
modernism
monarchy, the
Monophysite, Monophysitism
Montanism
Mormon, Mormonism (officially, the Church of Jesus Christ of Latter-Day Saints)
Mosaic
Mosaic Code (Pentateuch or Ten Commandments)
Mosaic Law (Pentateuch or Ten Commandments)
Most High God, the
Mount of Olives
Mount of Transfiguration, the
Mount Olivet Discourse (but Olivet discourse)
Mount Sinai
muezzin

mufti
Muhammad (preferred over
    Mohammad)
mullah
Muratorian Canon
Muslim (preferred over Moslem)
mystery
name of Christ, the
nativity of Christ, the
Nativity, the (the celebration)
Near East, Near Eastern
neoorthodox, neoorthodoxy
neo-Pentecostalism
neoplatonic, neoplatonism
New Age movement, the
new birth
New Covenant, the
    (New Testament)
new heaven and new earth
new Israel
New Jerusalem
New Testament church
New Thought (movement)
Nicene Creed
Nicene fathers
nonbiblical
non-Christian (n. and adj., but
    unchristian)
Nonconformists (religious
    movement)
nonliteral
North Galatian theory, the
northern kingdom (Israel)
NT
Nunc Dimittis

obeisance
occult, the
Old Covenant, the (Old
    Testament)
Olivet discourse (but Mount
    Olivet Discourse)
Omega, the
Omnipotent, the
One, the
one true God, the
Only Begotten, the
only begotten of the Father
only begotten Son of God
oracle (of doom, hope, etc.)
ordain, ordained, ordination
Order of Ministers
Order of Preachers (but the order,
    the Dominican order, etc.)
original sin
orthodox, orthodoxy
Orthodox Church, the
OT
Our Father, the (or the Lord's
    Prayer)
Oxford Group, the (movement,
    also known as Moral Re-
    Armament)
Oxford Movement
Palestine, Palestinian
Palestine covenant
Palm Sunday
papacy
papal infallibility
papyrus
parable of the prodigal son, the

Paraclete, the
paradise (Garden of Eden)
paradise (heaven)
Parousia, the
Paschal Lamb (Jesus)
Passion, the
Passion of Christ, the
Passion Sunday
Passion Week
Passover Feast, Seder
Passover Lamb (Jesus)
Passover, the
pastor, pastoral
Pastoral Epistles
Pastoral Letters
Paternoster (the Lord's Prayer)
patriarch, a
Patriarch, the (Abraham)
patriarchs, the (Hebrew)
patriarch, patriarchies
Patripassionism
patristic(s)
Paul, the apostle et al.
Paul's epistles
Paul's letters
Pauline Epistles
Peace, The (or The Kiss of Peace)
Pelagianism
penal substitution
penitence
Pentateuch, Pentateuchal
Pentecost
Pentecostal, Pentecostalism
people of God, the
Persia, Persian

person of Christ, the
Pesach (Passover)
Peshitta
Petrine
Pharaoh (without article, as a
    title)
pharaoh, the (general)
pharisaic (attitude)
Pharisaic (pertaining to the
    Pharisees)
Pharisee(s)
Pietism
piety, pietist(s), pietistic
Pilgrims, the
pillar of cloud
pillar of fire
plains of Moab
PLO (Palestinian Liberation
    Organization)
Poetic Books, the
polytheism
pontiff, the
pope, the
Pope John Paul II et al.
postbiblical
post-Christian
postexilic
postmillennial, postmillennial-
    ism, postmillennialist
post-Nicene fathers
posttribulation, posttribula-
    tional, posttribulationism,
    posttribulationist
pre-Christian
predestination

preexilic

premillenarian, premillenarian-
    ism

premillennial, premillennialism,
    premillennialist

premils

Presbyterian, Presbyterianism,
    Presbytery of Greater Atlanta
    et al.

presbytery (in a general sense)

Presence (God, Christ, or Holy
    Spirit)

presence (when used otherwise)

preterist(s)

pretribulation, pretribulational,
    pretribulationism, pretribula-
    tionist

priesthood of believers

priesthood of Christ

Prime Mover

Prince of Darkness

Prince of Peace

Prison Epistles

Prison Letters

proabortion, but pro-abortionist

pro-choice

Prodigal Son, the

pro-life

Promised Land, the

Promised One, the

promise-doctrine

promise-plan

proof-texts

prophet Isaiah (etc.), the

Prophet of Doom, the (Jeremiah,
    but Jeremiah was a prophet
    of doom)

Prophetic Books, the

Prophets, the (books of Old
    Testament)

prophets, the (people)

Protestant, Protestantism

Providence (as a name for God)

providence of God

Psalm 41, etc.

psalm, a

psalmist, the

Psalms, the (Old Testament)

psalter, a

Psalter, the (the Psalms)

pseudepigrapha, pseude-
    pigraphal

purgatory

Purim (Feast of Esther)

Puritan(s), Puritanism

pyx

Q (for Quelle)

Qoheleth (Hebrew for the
    teacher of wisdom)

Quakers (also known as the
    Society of Friends)

queen (but Queen of Sheba, etc.)

Quelle (German for source)

quietism

Qumran

Qumran Essenes

quo vadis? (Latin for where are
    you going?)

Qur'an (preferred, but also
    Qu'ran, Quran, Koran)

rabbi
rabbinic, rabbinical
Rahab
Ramadan
Ranters
Rapture, the (specific event)
rapture, the (doctrine of)
rapture of Christ (or the church)
Rastafarian, Rastafarianism
Real Presence (of Christ)
Received Text, the
reconciliation
Redeemer (Christ)
Redeemer-King
Reformation (Protestant)
reformation movement
Reformed Church in America
Reformed church(es)
Reformed theology
Reformers, the (specific group)
reincarnation
religion
Religious Right, the
remnant, the
Renaissance, the
Restoration, the (under Cyrus)
restoration movement
Resurrection, the
resurrection of Christ, the
resurrection of the body (of the
    dead, etc.)
revelation
Revelation (NT book)
Reverend (Smith, etc.)
reverend, reverence

righteous, righteousness
Rig-Veda
rite(s)
ritual
river (but capitalize when part
    of proper name: Jordan
    River)
Rock, the (Christ)
Roman Catholic Church
Roman Catholicism
Roman church
Roman Empire
Roman Rite
rosary, the
Rosh Hashanah, Hoshanah
    (Jewish New Year)
Rosicrucianism (movement)
Rule of Faith (Bible)
Ruler (God)
Sabbatarian, Sabbatarianism
sabbath (age)
Sabbath (day)
sabbatical (n. and adj.)
Sabellianism
sacerdotalism
sacrament(s)
sacramentalism, sacramentalist
Sacramentarian(ism)
Sacred Host
sacred rite(s)
sacrilege, sacrilegious
Sadducee(s)
Saint Peter et al.
saints, the
Salat al-fajr (special prayer)

Salvation Army
salvation history
salvific (adj.)
Samaria
Samaritan
sanctus
Sanhedrin
Satan
satanic, satanist, satanism
Savior
sayings of the wise
schism
Scholasticism
Scientology (movement)
scriptural
Scripture(s) (Bible, n. and adj.)
scripture(s) (other religions)
sea (capitalize when part of
    proper name: Red Sea, Sea of
    Galilee, etc.)
Second Adam, the (Christ)
Second Advent, the
Second Blessing, the
Second Coming, the
second coming of Christ, the
Second Great Awakening, the
second Joshua, the (Jesus)
Second Person of the Trinity
seder
Seekers, the
Selah (Hebrew liturgical notation)
Semi-Pelagianism
Semite, Semitic, Semitism
sensus plenior
Sephardic Jew

Sepuagesima
Septuagint (LXX)
seraph, seraphim
Sermon on the Mount
Serpent, the (Satan)
Seven Deadly Sins (pride, cov-
    etousness, lust, envy, glut-
    tony, anger, and sloth)
seven sacraments, the
Seventh-Day Adventist, Seventh-
    Day Adventism
Seventieth Week
Shabbat
Shabuoth (Pentecost)
Shakers, the
shalom
shalom aleichem
Shechina or Shekinh
Shema, the
Sheol
Shepherd Psalm, the
Shiite/Shi'ite
Shiloh
Shrove Tuesday
Shulammite
sign of the cross
sin offering
Sinai covenant, the
Sin-Bearer, the
Social Gospel
Society of Jesus (Jesuits)
Sola Fide
Sola Gratia
Sola Scriptura
Solomonic

Solomon's temple
son of David (Jesus)
Son of God (Jesus)
son of man (Ezekiel)
Son of Man (Jesus)
Song of Moses
Song of Songs (Solomon's)
sons of God (Christians)
sonship of Christ
soteriology
South Galatian theory, the
southern kingdom (Judah)
sovereign God
sovereign Lord
Spirit (when meaning the Holy
    Spirit; otherwise lowercase)
spirit of the age, the
spirit-guides
Star of David, the
stations of the cross
Stoicism (but *stoic* when used in
    a general sense)
Strangites, the
Sublapsarian
Subordinationism,
    Subordinationist
Suffering Servant
Sufi, Sufism
Sukkoth (Feast of Booths)
Sunday school (unless referring
    to a particular Sunday school,
    as in Walker Memorial
    Sunday School)
Sunna
Supralapsarian,

Supralapsarianism
Supreme Being, the
sutra
Swedenborgianism (movement,
    also known as the Church of
    the New Jerusalem)
synagogue
syncretism
synod (but Synod of Middle
    Tennessee, etc.)
Synoptic Gospels
Synoptic Problem, the
synoptics, the
Syriac
systematic theology
tabernacle, the (building)
table (the Lord's, etc.)
table of shewbread
Taliban, the
Talmud
Talmudic
Tanach
Tao, the (first principle of uni-
    verse)
Taoism (Chinese philosophy)
Targum
targumic
Te Deum Laudamus (Latin for
    We praise you, O God)
Teacher, the (*qoheleth*)
Teacher of Righteousness, the
Teacher of wisdom, the
    (*Qoheleth*)
tehillim (Hebrew for *praises*)
Temple, Solomonic

temple, the (at Jerusalem)
Temple Mount, the Mount
temple of the Lord, the
Temptation, the (Christ's)
temptation in the desert, the
temptation of Christ, the
Ten Articles, the (Anglican)
Ten Commandments (but the
    fifth commandment)
Ten Tribes, the
ten tribes of Israel, the
Tent of Meeting
Tent of the Testimony
tephillot (Hebrew for *prayers*)
Testaments, the
Tetragrammaton, the (YHWH)
Textus Receptus
theodicy
theology
theophany
Theophilus
Theosophical Society
Theosophy, theosophist
Thirty Years' War
Thirty-nine Articles, the
    (Anglican)
Thomist, Thomism
three persons of the Trinity, the
throne of grace, the
Thummim
Time of Jacob's Trouble, the
Time of the Gentiles, the
time of the judges, the
Torah
Tower of Babel

Transcendental Meditation (move-
    ment, also known as TM)
Transfiguration, the
transubstantiation
Trappists
Tree of Knowledge (of Good and
    Evil)
Tree of Life
tribe of Judah
Tribulation, the Great
Trinitarian, Trinitarianism
Trinity, the (but doctrine of the
    trinity)
Tripitaka
Triumphal Entry, the
triune God
Truth (the gospel, God's truth,
    ultimate truth)
Twelve, the (disciples)
twelve apostles, the
Twelve Articles, the
twelve prophets, the (minor
    prophets)
Twenty-third Psalm
Ugarit (kingdom of)
Ultramontanism
unchristian (but non-Christian)
un-Christlike
unction of the sick
underground church
ungodly
Unification Church, the
    (movement)
Unitarians (the Unitarian
    Universalist Association)

united kingdom (of Israel)

Unity School of Christianity, the (movement)

universal church

universalism

unlimited atonement

unscriptural

Upanishads

Upper Room, the

Upper Room Discourse

Urim

Vatican Council, First (Second)

Vedas, Vedic

Veneration of the Cross

Veneration of the Saints

venial sin

vestments

vestry

Via Dolorosa (Latin for *the sorrowful way*)

Via Egnatia (Egnatian Way)

viaticum; plural viaticums or viatica

Vicar of Christ (pope)

Vicar of Peter (pope)

Vicar, vicarage

Victor, the (Christ)

vigil

Vine, the (Christ)

Vinegar Bible

virgin birth, the

Virgin Mary, the

Vishnu

visible church

vocation

Voice, the (Holy Spirit)

Vulgate

Wailing Wall (Western Wall)

Waldenses, Waldensians

Water of Life (Christ)

Way, the (Christ)

Way International, the (movement)

(the) way, the truth, and the life

weltanschauung (German for *worldview*)

Wesleyanism

Western church

Western Rites

Western thought, etc.

Western Wall (Wailing Wall)

Westminster Catechism

Westminster Confession

Westminster Standards

Whitsunday (preferred, but also Whit Sunday)

Wicca

Wicked One, the (Satan)

will of God

Wisdom Literature, the

wise men (kings of the Orient who visited the Christ child)

Witness of the Spirit

Word, the (Bible or Christ)

Word made flesh (Christ)

Word of God (Bible)

Word of God (Christ)

Word of Life

Word of Truth

Work of Christ (salvation)

worldview
worshiped, worshiping, worshiper (preferable) OR worshipped, worshipping, worshipper
Writings, the
Yahrzeit
Yahweh, Yahwehwism, Yahwehwist, Yahwehwistic (or YHWH or YHVH)
yarmulke
Year of Jubilee
YHWH (or YHVH)
Yoga (Hindu system)
Yom Kippur (Day of Atonement)
Young Men's Christian Association (YMCA)
Young Women's Christian Association (YWCA)
yuletide
zealot, zealotry, zealousness
Zebulun
zeitgeist
Zen
Zen Buddhism
Zeus
ziggurat
Zion, Zionism, Zionist
zodiac
Zoroaster, Zoroastrian, Zoroasterianism
Zwinglianism

CHAPTER 6

Footnotes and References for General Audiences (16.1–.120)

A. General Rules

It is the author's responsibility to provide complete and accurate footnotes as part of the manuscript prior to its undergoing the editorial process.

1. Number footnotes consecutively throughout each chapter of the book, beginning with the number 1 in each new chapter.

2. Type the footnotes on sheets separate from the text. Double-space them with generous margins.

3. In published form, notes are usually printed at the end of the book, not at the end of each chapter or at page bottoms. The publisher will make the decision about the appropriate place to put them. In the disk/printout given

to the publisher, the notes should appear at chapter ends or at the end of the book—not in a footnote window.

4. Each footnote for a book should include the following information:

> Author's full name
>
> Complete title of book
>
> Editor, compiler, or translator, if any
>
> Edition, if other than the first
>
> Number of volumes
>
> Facts of publication—city where published, publisher, date of publication
>
> Volume number (if any)
>
> Page number(s) of the particular citation (Omit the abbreviations *p.* or *pp.* from the citations.)

5. When citing an article from a periodical as the source, the following information should appear:

> Author's full name
>
> Title of the article
>
> Name of the periodical
>
> Volume (and number) of the periodical
>
> Date of the volume or issue
>
> Page number(s) of the particular citation (Again, omit the abbreviations *p.* or *pp.* in the citations.)

6. After the first reference to a particular work in each chapter, subsequent references in the same chapter should be in shortened formats. The shortened reference should include only the last name of the author and the short title of the book in italics or of the magazine/journal article enclosed in quotation marks, followed by the page numbers of the reference.

1. Harold G. Henderson, *An Introduction to Haiku: An Anthology of Poems and Poets from Basho to Shiki* (New York: Doubleday Anchor Books, 1958), 124.

2. A. L. Clauson, "Religious Imagery in Dylan's Later Songs," *Poetry and Christianity* 15 (Summer 2001), 110.

3 Fyodor Dostoevsky, *The Possessed* (New York: Signet Classics, 1962), 224.

4. Henderson, *An Introduction to Haiku*, 78.

5. Clauson, "Religious Imagery in Dylan's Later Songs," 112.

7. *Ibid.* is acceptable for referring to a single work cited in the note immediately preceding. It takes the place of the author's name, the title of the work, and the succeeding identical material. Incidentally, use Roman type for Latin words and abbreviations in footnotes: Ibid., et al., op cit., inter alia, idem.

11. C. S. Lewis, *The Allegory of Love: A Study in Medieval Tradition* (Oxford: Clarendon Press, 1936), 259.

12. Ibid., 360.

B. Internet References (17.180–.187, 17.234–.37)

Citing from the Internet is a relatively new area in scholarship. We suggest caution in quoting from Web-based sources, as it is difficult to verify the level of expertise or credentials behind some of the information available online. Follow the general rules for citing sources in books or periodicals, attempting to be as complete as possible. Following are some examples:

1. C. E. Ediger, "You Can't Kid a Quilter," from "Quilting Graffiti," *Quilters Anonymous* online magazine, from *Quilting Monthly* (2 December 2001), quiltingmonthly.com/anonymous/graffiti.

2. Ken Stephens and David Shepherd, "A Brief History of Nashville Publishing," About.com, 20 April 2000 (accessed June 20, 2001).

3. Shawn L. Stanford, "A Meeting of the Minds: Creation of the Arizona Constitution," Web-based article taken from the Introduction to *Liberty and Justice: The Writing of the Arizona State Constitution* (Phoenix: Published for the Arizona Constitutional Preservation Administration by the State of Arizona Archives Trust Fund Board, Arizona Archives and Records Foundation, 1998), http:www.azconst.gov.

C. Scripture References (8.111–.115, 17.246–.249)

1. It is the author's responsibility to provide accurate and complete references to the Bible.

2. Do not abbreviate books of the Bible when you cite a reference without specific chapter and verse.

> Deuteronomy is one of the first five books of the Bible commonly known as the Pentateuch.

3. In a citation in block quotations, it is proper form to abbreviate the names of Bible books. (See chapter 3, "Elements of Style," Section D, "Abbreviations and Scripture References.")

4. Use Arabic numerals to cite all references to Scripture.

> 1 Chronicles   2 Peter   3 John

5. It is acceptable to abbreviate the names of Bible versions when citing a reference. (See chapter 3, "Elements of Style," Section D, "Abbreviations and Scripture References.")

6. When quoting Scripture, place the period after the parentheses containing the reference. If the quotation ends in a question or exclamation point, place it with the text and place a period after the last parenthesis.

> "Finally, my brothers, rejoice in the Lord" (Phil. 3:1).

> "'If I want him to remain until I come,' Jesus answered, 'what is that to you?'" (John 21:21).

CHAPTER 7
Academic Style Requirements

A. General Style Rules for Academic Books

1. Quotations must be exact. If you quote from a version that uses a specific convention, follow the same convention as your source: "Lord" often appears as LORD in the NIV, for example. Watch for deity capitalization conventions in your chosen version and follow that convention when quoting verses or passages.

2. Place a period at the end of Bible block quotations (after the book, chapter, and verse reference).

3. In footnotes, endnotes, or backnotes, *ed.* (editor) should appear after the editor's name, not before.

4. Capitalize all titles for Christ, even if they do not appear in the capitalization list in this book: Creator, Redeemer, Lord, Savior, Messiah, and so on.

5. Capitalize major movements or schools of thought (e.g., Rationalism, Pietism, Romanticism, Idealism).

6. Capitalize names of specific major religions like Christianity, or Buddhism but do not capitalize names of religions or religious systems that are general terms, like animism, spiritism, or monotheism.

7. Capitalize the names of major biblical covenants (e.g., Abrahamic Covenant, Davidic Covenant). Also capitalize Old Covenant and New Covenant.

8. Do not capitalize the word "book" in phrases like "the book of Genesis."

9. Use an abbreviation for the name of a biblical book when writing book, chapter, *and* verse, with no period after the abbreviation (e.g., Jer 31:31). But write out the complete name of the book when citing only book and chapter (e.g., Jeremiah 31).

10. Do not italicize abbreviations such as the following: e.g., i.e., cf.

11. In academic books, most publishers advise writers not to capitalize pronouns that you use to refer to God (e.g., his, not His), and not to capitalize words like "biblical" and "scriptural." The only exceptions to these rules are occasions when you are directly quoting someone who capitalizes them or when you are quoting from a version of the Bible that capitalizes them (see above).

12. Except in quotations, Old Testament should be written OT and New Testament should be written NT.

13. In footnotes, endnotes, or backnotes when referring to page numbers, be sure to include p. or pp. before the numbers (e.g., pp. 102–112, not 102–112). The only exceptions are initial references to pages in a journal or magazine article, such as *Journal of Religious Thought* 17 March 1996: 8–15.

14. Use the abbreviations for journals as listed in works such as *Guide to Religious Periodical Literature* and *Philosophers Index*.

15. Do not capitalize major areas of theology like bibliology, anthropology, christology, soteriology, and eschatology.

16. Capitalize adjectives that refer to nationalities like American, Canadian, British, and French.

17. Whenever using a Hebrew or Greek word, transliterate it in accord with the Society for Biblical Literature specifications for transliteration as published in *The SBL Handbook of Style for Ancient New Eastern, Biblical, and Early Christian Studies* (Peabody, Mass.: Hendrickson Publishers, Inc., 1999). In special cases there may be a need to use the original Hebrew and Greek, but such cases will be determined by mutual agreement of the publisher and the author.

B. Bible Book Abbreviations for Academic Books

Old Testament

Gen	1 Sam	Esth	Lam	Mic
Exod	2 Sam	Job)	Ezek	Nah
Lev	1 Kgs	Ps(s)	Dan	Hab
Num	2 Kgs	Prov	Hos	Zeph
Deut	1 Chr	Eccl	Joel	Hag
Josh	2 Chr	Song	Amos	Zech
Judg	Ezra	Isa	Obad	Mal
Ruth	Neh	Jer	Jonah	

New Testament

Matt	Eph	Heb
Mark	Phil	Jas
Luke	Col	1 Pet
John	1 Thess	2 Pet
Acts	2 Thess	1 John
Rom	1 Tim	2 John
1 Cor	2 Tim	3 John
2 Cor	Titus	Jude
Gal	Phlm	Rev

These abbreviations do not require a period and are not italicized.

CHAPTER 8
Words, Words, Words— Tricky Spellings and Meanings, Bugaboos, and Pitfalls

Watch out for the following disputed issues, fallacies, tricky or confusing terms, and misused words. It is usually helpful to keep a good grammar textbook handy as a reference for questionable words, usage, or punctuation; there probably is not an editor's bookshelf in the country that doesn't have several such references. In some instances, however, the grammar books may not agree with this style guide or with *The Chicago Manual of Style, Fifteenth Edition;* in these cases, the author should follow the style of the publishing house. See the many excellent resources listed in chapter 12 of this style book, entitled "Suggested Books for Authors and Editors."

a lot Never *alot.*

a/an before "H" words Usage depends on whether the *h* is pronounced. We would not call something "an historical event" just as we would not say "an home run." We would, however, call someone "an honest person," because the *h* is silent.

-able Generally the silent *e* is dropped when adding the suffix *-able* to a verb (livable), unless the suffix comes after a soft *g* (manageable) or sibilant *c* (peaceable). When a verb ends in a consonant and a *y*, change the *y* to *i* before adding -able (justifiable). When a verb ends in -ate, drop the syllable before adding -able (demonstrable).

abridged/expurgated/unabridged *Abridged* implies reduction. *Expurgated* has the sense of purging or cleansing. An expurgated book is one in which certain passages have been removed. *Unabridged* means "not reduced in scope by omitting anything."

abstruse/obscure/obtuse An idea that is *abstruse* is difficult to understand or explain; it is concealed. Something that is *obscure* is either relatively unknown or uncertain or not clearly seen or distinguished. *Obtuse* (not *obstruse*) means blunt, dull, or not sharp or pointed. (An obtuse angle is an angle that measures more than 90 degrees and less than 180 degrees.) Another sense of obtuse is insensitivity or stupidity—lacking in sharpness or quickness of intellect.

accept/except The former means "to receive," "to agree with," "to say yes to." The latter, as a verb, means "to omit" or "to exclude," while as a preposition it means "other than."

acronym/acrostic An *acronym* is a word formed from the initial letters of other words. The word is often a short, easy to remember name for an organization whose official name is longer: MADD for "Mothers Against

Drunk Driving." There are other acronyms, however, that are names for something but are not words in the traditional sense: FBI and USA, for example. An *acrostic* is a word puzzle where the first or last letters of each line form a word or words.

active consideration A cliché; use *thinking it over* instead.

acute/chronic *Chronic* means constant and lasting. It is the opposite of *acute,* which applies to an illness or situation that is approaching a crisis or critical stage.

AD/AH/AS/BC/BCE/CE Abbreviations for eras are set in full capitals with no periods. AD should always precede the year number (i.e., AD 33), but it should go after the century (third century AD). BC should always go after the year (40 BC). BCE ("before the common era") and CE ("of the common era") are sometimes used instead of AD and BC, but most Christian publishing houses prefer the latter designation referring to the Advent of Christ.

ad hoc Literally, "toward this." An ad hoc committee is one appointed to take care of a specific case or problem.

address Address a letter, not a problem. Instead, deal with, take up, consider, tackle, or cope with a problem.

adverse/averse The first means unfavorable ("He received an adverse report") or hostile ("The game was stopped by adverse weather"); the second means unwilling or disinclined ("I was averse to publishing the book").

advice/advise *Advice* is a noun and means "an opinion" or "a recommendation." *Advise* is a verb and has the basic meaning of "to counsel," "to give advice to," and also "to inform." ("B&H advises writers to follow our usage advice.")

affect/effect These are not synonyms. *Effect* as a verb is a way of saying "bring about" or "produce" (as in "effect a change"). As a noun, *effect* means the change *effected* in something by whatever has *affected* it. As a verb, *affect* means to influence ("Smoking will affect one's health") or to adopt a pose or manner ("He affected ignorance"). Avoid the noun *affect,* for it has a narrow psychological meaning that few are likely to understand. As a noun, *effect* is the word almost always needed.

affluent/effluent Both adjectives have reference to streams or any flowing liquids. An *affluent* stream flows into something; an *effluent* one flows out from a source. The same stream can be affluent from the point of view of one observer and effluent from that of another. Affluent is also used in the sense of flowing in abundance, having an increasing supply, and rich.

African American/black *The Chicago Manual of Style, Fifteenth Edition* recommends using either as an ethnic term. Keep in mind that the term *black* is now often not capitalized as the widely accepted name for the dark-skinned group or groups of people originating in Africa (just as the term *white* is often not capitalized as the preferred term for light-skinned people). *Negro* is a reputable term, but many blacks do not prefer it. Note: African American, not Afro-American.

aggravate/irritate *Aggravate* means to exasperate or to make a bad situation worse; *irritate* means to vex or annoy. Only circumstances can be aggravated, never people.

AH Anno Hebraica, in the Hebrew year. The proper format is full capital letters. See **AD/AH/AS/BC/BCE/CE.**

AIDS/HIV (Not Aids or AIDS) follows the same convention, with no periods between the letters.

aisle/isle The first is a passage between seats; the second is an island.

albeit An archaic term.

allegory/fable/legend/myth/parable Both *fables* and *parables* are stories intended to have instructional value. They differ in that parables are concerned with religious or ethical themes, while fables usually entail more practical considerations. *Allegories* are metaphors, narratives where the principal characters represent things that are not explicitly stated. *Myths* are stories designed to explain a belief or a phenomenon, but a more current meaning of myth is as an invented story or a popular misconception. *Legends* are traditions or stories handed down from earlier times and now popularly accepted as true or believable.

all right Never *alright.*

allude/elude The former means to make an indirect reference or to refer to something by way of implication or suggestion. The latter means to avoid, evade, or escape. One alludes to a verse of Scripture but eludes a dangerous situation.

allusion/delusion/illusion An *allusion* is an indirect reference that is not specifically mentioned (so that the readers are left to make their own judgments about what you are implying); a *delusion* is a false belief or opinion; and an *illusion* is a false or unreal image or a misunderstanding of reality.

along with/together with In these expressions, *with* is a preposition, not a conjunction. As a preposition, it does not govern the verb. Therefore, these expressions require a singular verb. ("The publisher, together with the editor arrested earlier for assaulting the author, was questioned.")

altar/alter An *altar* is a table or block used in religious worship. *Alter* means to change.

alternately/alternatively *Alternately* means by turns, as in "He traveled alternately by bus, train, and airplane." *Alternatively* means available in place of something else, as in "He decided to travel by train, or alternatively, by bus."

although/though Except at the end of sentences where only *though* is correct, these words are interchangeable.

AM/PM or **a.m./p.m.** These abbreviations can be set in regular capital letters without periods, or they can be set in lowercase with periods.

amid(st)/among *Among* applies to things that can be separated and counted, *amid* to things that cannot. One works *among* the poor, but one works *amidst* poverty. Either *amid* or *amidst* is correct.

among/between Usually *between* includes the notion of "two," whereas *among* should not be used with fewer than three things. Nevertheless, St. Louis is *between* California, New York, and Michigan, not *among* them. Where the words can be distinguished, apply *between* to reciprocal arrangements (a treaty between the United States and Canada) and *among* to collective arrangements (trade talks among members of the European community). Remember that when forced to choose between (or among) alternative usages, none of which sounds right, consider that the problem with the sentence may not be its use of *between* or *among* but rather its simple clarity in general.

amoral/immoral The first applies to matters beyond the moral order or to questions where morality does not arise. The second applies to evil things.

and/or Do not use the sometimes confusing shortcut of "and/or."

androcentric/gynecocentric A *gynecocentric* society is one dominated by women, or a society where the female point of view is dominant. An *androcentric* society, in contrast, means male centered.

answer/reply/response An *answer* is something said or written or done. A *reply* is an answer that satisfies in detail a question asked or a charge made, or the like. A *response* is an appropriate reaction to a stimulus.

antecedence/antecedents *Antecedence* means priority or precedence. *Antecedents* are ancestors or things or circumstances that have gone before.

anticipate/expect A clear distinction should be kept between these words. When one *expects*, one "looks ahead to" ("I expect it to rain"). But to *anticipate* means to look ahead to and then do something about it ("I put the car in the garage, anticipating rain").

antique/antiques Both a noun and an adjective. An antique is a rare object or one that belongs to the distant past. But for stores or people who trade in old objects, it is antiques store or antiques dealer.

anybody Do not write as two words. The same is true for *anyone, everybody, nobody,* and *somebody.*

any more/anymore When you are writing about something additional, make it two words. "She refused any more advice from him." As an adverb, one word. "The editor didn't want to argue with the author anymore."

appraise/apprise *Appraise* means to evaluate the value or quality of a thing; *apprise* means to inform.

AS Anno Salutis, in the Year of Salvation. The proper format is regular capital letters and no periods. See **AD/AH/AS/BC/BCE/CE.**

as/like *As* and *as if* are usually followed by a verb; *like* almost never is. See **like/as.**

Asian The correct term for people of Asian ancestry is *Asian,* not "Asiatic" and not "Oriental."

aught/ought *Aught* means anything, any little part, or in any respect: "For aught I care, you can jump in the lake." *Ought* has to do with duty or obligation: "I ought to be by her side." See **naught/nought.**

aural/oral *Aural* has to do with the ear or the sense of hearing. *Oral* is by mouth or spoken; when linked to communication, it refers to human speech.

averse/adverse See **adverse/averse.**

awhile Considered by many to be a breach of proper or normal form. If used, best used as the object of a preposition, as in "She sold Avon products for awhile" (even though the idea of *for* is implicit in *awhile*). Almost always better to use two words, **a while.**

baboonery/buffoonery *Baboonery* suggests conduct that is clownish and grotesque and perhaps cruel. *Buffoonery* is playful or foolish behavior.

bail/bale *Bail* is money or property pledged as security, a prisoner's bond, but one also bails out (scoops water out of) a boat or bails out (jumps from) of an air-plane. A *bale* is a bundle of cotton, straw, or hay. The rarely used word *bale* is also a great evil, misfortune, misery, or sorrow; usually it appears in adjectival form: a baleful expression.

bare/bear The former means not covered or without decoration. As a noun, the latter is a large or medium-sized furry animal, a bad-tempered person, a difficult thing that is hard to tolerate or endure, or a bad business market. As a verb, *bear* is to hold or support something, to merit or be worthy of something, to accept something as a duty or responsibility, or to be marked by something.

bathos The sudden appearance of triteness or extreme sentimentality into an otherwise elevated discussion or style. See also **clichés** and **purple passages**.

BC/AD/BCE/AH/AS/CE See **AD/AH/AS/BC/BCE/CE**.

belles lettres Literary studies and writings. Usually treated as a plural.

between/among See **among/between**.

between you and me Not "between you and I."

biannual/biennial *Biannual* means that something happens twice a year. *Biennial* means that something happens every second year.

bibliomania/bibliophilism *Bibliophilism* describes a love of books, especially for the quality of their format. *Bibliomania* means an extreme preoccupation with collecting books. Other related terms include *biblia abiblia*, worthless books on literature; *bibliobibuli*, people who read too much and have no other interests; *biblioclast*, a destroyer or mutilator of books; *bibliofilm*, microfilm used for photographing pages of books; *bibliogony,* the production of books; *biblioklept,* one who steals books; *bibliolatry,* the excessive liking of books; *bibliopegy,* the art and craft of bookbinding; *bibliomancy,* divination by books; *bibliophage,* a bookworm or anything else that eats or devours books; *bibliophobia,* the fear of books; *bibliopole,* a bookseller, *bibliotaph,* one who hoards books; and, *bibliotheca,* a library.

bibliotherapy Denis Diderot in 1781 claimed to have cured his wife from depression by reading (raunchy literature) to her, thus starting the new science that would later be called *bibliotherapy.*

bibliotics The study of handwriting, writing materials, and written documents to determine authenticity and authorship.

billion/trillion In the United States and Great Britain, a billion signifies one thousand million (1,000,000,000), but in France and Germany it signifies one million million (1,000,000,000,000). In the United States and Great Britain, a trillion signifies one million million, but in France and Germany it is one million million million (1,000,000,000,000,000,000).

bite/byte As a verb, *bite* means to apply teeth to. As a noun, it is what the teeth have been applied to, or the act of applying them (taking a bite). A *byte,* however, is a computer term for units of information storage.

black/African American See **African American/black**.

bogey/bogie/bogy *Bogey* is a golf term, but it is also used in another way for a ghostly or devilish figure. *Bogy* is also used in both ways. Neither should be confused with *bogie,* wheels on the railway.

born/borne The former has to do only with the idea of birth ("I was born in 1947"). The latter is used for the sense of supporting or tolerating ("He has borne the burden with great dignity") and also in active constructions for giving birth ("Sylvia has borne six children") and in passive constructions ("The six children borne by her").

(the) bottom line Many use this to sound technical, but instead they sound typical. "The bottom line" is an extremely overworked and ordinary term that should not be used outside of the technical field of accounting (where it is the line at the bottom of a financial report showing the net profit or loss). In running text, try using words like conclusion, consequence, crux, culmination, decision, denouement, effect, end, end result, essence, essential thing, final analysis, final result, input, key, keynote, main point, outcome, parameters, pragmatic, primary consideration, realistic, result, salient point, or upshot.

brake/break *Brake,* a noun, is a device that slows or stops the progress of something, or acts as a restraint on something ("The brake on book sales is attributed to the lagging economy"). *Break* is a verb that means to separate or damage something ("to break in two"), to finish something ("The conservatives broke their relationship with the liberals"), to suddenly start something ("The storm broke"), or to interrupt something ("The noise will break my train of thought").

breach/breech A *breach* is the breaking of a rule or an estrangement, while a *breech* means the rear part or lower portion of anything.

bring/take Usually, *bring* implies motion toward the speaker or a place associated with the speaker; it suggests "to come here with." *Take* usually implies motion away from the speaker or place; it suggests "to go there with."

byte/bite See **bite/byte**.

Cadmean victory/Pyrrhic victory A victory that leaves the victor ruined is a *Cadmean* victory. A victory won at too excessive a cost is a *Pyrrhic* victory.

calendar/calender The first is a chart showing the record of a particular year, and the second is a type of machine press that uses rollers to glaze and smooth cloth or paper.

can Do not use this as a substitute for *may*.

cannon/canon A *cannon* is a large gun that fires solid metal balls; *canon* refers to a body of sacred, religious writings accepted as genuine, or to the works of a particular author. Rarely it is the title for a specific type of clergyman. Canon law is church law. Canon can also refer to a type of musical composition.

cant/jargon *Cant* has derogatory implications because it is considered insincere talk; it applies to the private vocabulary or expressions of professions and social groups. *Jargon* does not have the same derogatory overtones as *cant*; it suggests terms used in a particular group or profession that are hard for outsiders to understand.

canvas/canvass The former is a fabric; the latter means to solicit, especially for votes.

cardinal numbers/ordinal numbers Cardinal numbers: one, two, three, etc. Ordinal numbers: first, second, third, etc.

cease/seize The former means stop; the latter means grab or capture.

ceiling/sealing The top of a room (and also the upper limit of a budget, etc.) is the *ceiling*; *sealing*, however, is the waterproofing or covering up of seals.

celebrant/celebrator A *celebrant* is one who participates in a religious ceremony, while a *celebrator* is one who engages in revelry.

celibacy/chastity *Celibacy* means only to be unmarried and does not necessarily indicate abstinence from sex, which is *chastity*.

cement/concrete As *cement* is a constituent of *concrete*, the terms are not interchangeable.

cemetery Not –*ary*.

censer/censor/censure A *censer* is a vessel for burning incense; a *censor* is an official who suppresses books and other written material; and, *censure* is disapproval.

cent/scent/sent Small change is a *cent*. Perfume has a *scent*. *Sent* is from the verb *to send*.

Chanukah Interchangeable with Hanuka and Hanukkah.

charisma *Charisma* should be reserved as a theological term for the special grace that empowers. Unless this is meant, use appeal, magnetism, attractiveness, etc.

cheap/cheep The first is low priced; the second is a bird sound.

chord/cord A *chord* is a combination of musical notes sounded together in harmony. It is also used for a straight line joining two points on a curve. A *cord* is a length of rope or other connector. A cord can also be a spiritual, emotional or moral bond.

chronic/acute See **acute/chronic**.

cite/site To *cite* is to quote or mention. As a noun, a *site* is ground on which a building stands; as a verb, it means to position or be positioned.

clan/extended family/nuclear family/tribe *Nuclear family* refers to one's immediate family; specifically, father, mother, and their children. *Extended family* includes the nuclear family and adds grandparents and other close relatives. A *clan* is a family that goes beyond close relatives to include uncles, aunts, cousins, etc. If relationship is not considered, you have a *tribe*.

classic/classical *Classic* means something of the first rank or of the highest class. *Classical* refers to the art and culture of Greek and Roman antiquity.

clever This word has a different meaning when applied to animals than it does when applied to humans. A clever animal is a good-natured one. A clever person is ingenious.

clichés Because of the gleeful appropriation of colorful words and phrases by the media, newly coined ways of expressing ideas can quickly become clichés. The following words and phrases are examples of the kinds of words or phrases that are in danger of becoming overused: 24/7, been there–done that, bottom line, changing your paradigm, color outside the box, cutting edge, cut to the chase, don't go there, downsizing, each and every one, if you fail to plan–plan to fail, lifestyle, like a bolt of lightening, like a ton of bricks, living on the edge, mother of all . . . , new paradigm, no brainer, out of the box, quantum leap, reengineering, rightsizing, sink without a ripple, smoking gun, stuck out like a sore thumb, synergy, tsunami, where the rubber meets the road. Be cautious when using terms that seem to have come into vogue overnight; just as quickly they can become trite.

coat/cote The former is a garment or animal's outer covering and also applies to the application of paint. The latter is a bird or animal shelter.

coequal Pointless word. Use *equal*.

college/university In American usage, one goes *to* college and *to the* university.

commiseration/compassion/empathy/pity/sympathy *Commiseration* suggests less emotion than compassion but more emotion than pity. *Compassion* is a deeply felt understanding of the problems of others. *Empathy* denotes a close understanding of the feelings of another, vicariously putting oneself in another's place. *Pity,* more condescending, suggests understanding a problem intellectually but not necessarily emotionally. *Sympathy* is a general feeling of harmony or agreement between persons and is a less specific word than the others.

common-gender pronouns The lack of a common-gender pronoun in English has led to some interesting experimental monstrosities, such as "heshe" for he or she, "s/he" for she or he, "himer" for him or her, "hiser" for his or her, and "himerself" for himself or herself. Of course, these would sound too strange to be used in speech, and as they deviate so dramatically from normal language, they should not be used in formal writing. See **nonsexist use of language**.

compassion/commiseration/empathy/pity/sympathy See **commiseration/compassion/empathy/pity/sympathy**.

compendium A *compendium* is an abridgment that offers a complete summary in a brief way. It does not mean vast and all-embracing.

complementary/complimentary *Complementary* refers to filling out or completing, making up a whole or balance ("She complements him in every way"). *Complimentary* means giving praise ("The book received complimentary reviews") or giving away something for free as a service or a courtesy ("A complimentary copy of *The Little Style Guide to Great Christian Writing and Publishing* is given to all our lucky authors").

composed of/divided into Do not confuse these. A piece of fruit can be divided into halves, but the fruit itself is composed of skin, pulp, and seeds.

comprise/constitute *Comprise* means to contain, to include, or to embrace. *Constitute* means to form or to make up. A zoo comprises animals, but animals constitute a zoo.

concrete/cement See **cement/concrete**.

consensus (Not *concensus*) Agreement. Do not say "consensus of opinion," which is redundant.

contagious/infectious *Contagious* describes diseases spread on contact or by close association. Diseases are *infectious* if they spread through air or water. As an adjective, infectious can also apply to other things that can spread quickly, such as fear.

contrary/converse/opposite/reverse *Contrary* is a statement that contradicts a proposition. A *converse* reverses the elements of a proposition. An *opposite* is something diametrically opposed to a proposition. *Reverse* can mean all of these things.

convince/persuade *Convince* requires a state of the mind, while *persuade* requires a course of action. We convince people to believe but persuade them to act.

cooperate Do not hyphenate.

coordinate Do not hyphenate.

cote/coat See **coat/cote**.

council/counsel A body of legislators or advisors is a *council*, but advice or the act of giving advice (especially legal) is *counsel*.

creationism/creationist The doctrine of *creationism* holds that all matter was created out of nothing by an omnipotent God. A *creationist* is a person who believes creationism.

creole/pidgin A system of speech that is devised by two or more peoples who share no common language is called a *pidgin* language. A *creole* is a language spoken by those for whom a pidgin language is their first tongue. As such, a creole is a more evolved and formal language than a pidgin.

crevasse/crevice A deep fissure, as in ice, is a *crevasse*, but a narrow and shallow one is a *crevice*.

cryptonym/pseudonym A *cryptonym* is a pseudonym that is kept secret from all but a few persons. A *pseudonym* is a "false name" or a "pen" name that an author uses.

cumber/encumber The first means to hinder; the second also means to hinder or impede some activity, but it is used as well in the sense of weighing down or burdening.

cyclone/hurricane/tornado/tsunami/whirlwind A *cyclone* is a storm or wind system that rotates around a center of low pressure and moves in a rotating formation. A *tornado* is a violent, destructive whirling wind that includes a funnel-shaped cloud and moves along a narrow path; *whirlwind* is a close synonym for *tornado*. A *hurricane* is a tropical cyclone that starts over an ocean. A *tsunami* is a large destructive ocean wave.

dangling participles A common bugaboo in less than careful writing. Example: "Standing on the hotel room balcony, the sun immediately made Carol feel warm." This construction implies that the sun is standing on the balcony. Rather, the sentence should read, "Standing on the hotel room balcony, Carol immediately felt the warmth of the sun." Another example: "Completing the graduate theater studies program, David's acting career began." This sentence sounds as if the acting career actually completed the graduate program. The sentence should read, "Completing the graduate theater studies program, David began his acting career." Make sure that the participial phrase refers to the person, place, or thing actually doing the action, rather than "dangling" unsupported in the sentence.

data "The data is irrelevant" is not correct. Remember that *data* is plural.

day in and day out A worn-out phrase. Try other expressions, such as always, constantly, continually, endlessly, every day, forever, frequently, nonstop, perpetually, persistently, or unceasingly.

deep six To get rid of something. The expression probably refers to putting something under six fathoms of water.

defuse/diffuse To *defuse* means to make harmless; *diffuse* is to spread out widely or thinly or to disperse.

delusion/allusion/illusion See **allusion/delusion/illusion**.

demise Death; not the same as decline.

depositary/depository One entrusted with goods is a *depositary*, while the place where goods are stored is a *depository*.

desert/deserts/dessert One "s" can make a lot of difference. *Desert* refers to arid barren land. As a verb, to *desert* means to abandon. When writing of those deserving reward or punishment, use the word *deserts,* as in "They got their just deserts." A *dessert* is a sweet dish usually served at the end of a meal.

device/devise A *device* is a design or a contrivance. To *devise* is to invent or to plan.

differ from/differ with To *differ from* means to be unlike. To *differ with* means to disagree.

different to/from/than *Different to* and *different from* are considered standard English. *Different to* follows the pattern of "similar to," while *different from* contrasts different things. *Different than* is not considered standard English, although it is unobjectionable in terms of its grammar. "Writers are different from (not than) editors."

diffuse/defuse See **defuse/diffuse**.

dilemma Not a synonym for predicament or jam or trouble. Rather, *dilemma* refers to someone facing two alternative courses of action, both of which are likely to be unpleasant.

disassemble/dissemble *Dissemble* means to pretend or disguise one's true feelings or motives, but *disassemble* means to take apart.

discreet/discrete *Discreet* means circumspect, with propriety, and showing good judgment. *Discrete* means in separate parts.

disenfranchise/disfranchise These words are interchangeable.

disinterested/uninterested The first means neutral,

unbiased, or personally detached; the second means not interested in or not caring.

disregardless/irregardless Both are incorrect. Use *regardless* or *irrespective*.

dissemble/disassemble See **disassemble/dissemble**.

divided into/composed of See **composed of/divided into**.

dogma/dogmatic Religious beliefs and tenets prescribed by a church (or even a political order) constitute *dogma*. A person who is *dogmatic* holds to certain opinions or beliefs and is not willing to accept any others.

dos and don'ts Not *do's*.

dual/duel *Dual* means twofold; a *duel* is a fight between two persons.

each When *each* precedes the noun or pronoun to which it refers, make the verb singular: "Each of us was . . ." When it follows the noun or pronoun, however, the verb should be plural: "They each were . . ."

each other/one another *Each other* for two things; *one another* for more than two.

effect/affect See **affect/effect**.

effluent/affluent See **affluent/effluent**.

e.g./i.e. Don't confuse these abbreviations. *E.g.* stands for *exempli gratia,* "for the sake of example," while *i.e.* stands for *id est,* "that is." Do not italicize.

egest/ingest *Ingest* means to take substances such as food and drink into the body. *Egestion* refers to sweating and exhaling and to excreting waste from the digestive tract.

eisegesis/exegesis *Eisegesis* explains written or printed material, but it emphasizes the interpreter's own beliefs and theories and not what the text actually says. *Exegesis* means the careful, detailed explaining of written or printed material, usually the Bible.

either Use a singular verb if the noun or pronoun nearest the verb is singular: "Either Kim or John is going to edit the manuscript." Use a plural verb if the noun or pronoun nearest the verb is plural: "Either David or the board of directors are going to have the last word."

elegy/eulogy An *elegy* is a mournful poem. A *eulogy* is a tribute to the dead.

elude/allude See **allude/elude**.

e-mail Do not capitalize. See **chapter 9, "Publishing and Technology Helps," Section D, "Electronic Media Terms."**

emasculate/enervate/unman/unnerve To *emasculate* refers to the taking away of a fundamental force by removing something essential. ("The courts have emasculated the powers of the police.") To *enervate* is to reduce one's energy or vigor; the past perfect, *enervated*, is commonly used as an adjective. ("After mowing the lawn in the noonday sun, he felt enervated.") The verb *unman* implies a loss of manly spirit, vigor, or fortitude. ("He was unmanned by the noise of the thief in the night.") It can also be an adjective meaning not manned (as in an unmanned space flight). To *unnerve* implies the taking away of strength or vigor and depriving one of effective action. ("She was unnerved when she saw her stalker.")

empathy/compassion/pity/commiseration/sympathy See **commiseration/compassion/empathy/pity/sympathy**.

encumber/cumber See **cumber/encumber**.

endemic/epidemic/pandemic A disease is *epidemic* when it spreads rapidly and when it afflicts many people in a specific area, but it is *pandemic* if it is widespread and affects a large proportion of the people. When a disease is long-standing and found only in a particular place or among a particular people, it is *endemic*. *Endemic* can also refer to an idea or characteristic that is prevalent or specific to a set of beliefs.

enquiry/inquiry In the United States *inquiry* and *inquire* are preferred over *enquiry* and *enquire*. See **query/inquiry/enquiry**.

especial/special *Especial* means to a high degree; *special* means for a particular purpose.

etc. Do not use this abbreviation in textual discourse; instead, use a phrase such as "and similar approaches" or "and other ideas"; do not spell out *et cetera* as a way of completing a list.

ethics/morality The former is used mostly when the conduct of all or a large part of society is under discussion. The latter is used mostly when a particular person, religion, group, or profession is under discussion. It is also used to refer to a system of moral principles, such as "legal ethics" or "theological ethics" or "medical ethics."

eugenics/euthenics The former has to do with improving humans (or animals and plants) through controlling reproduction. One who believes in *euthenics,* however, thinks that human improvement must come basically from betterment of environment.

eulogy/elegy See **elegy/eulogy**.

everyday/every day The first is an adjective ("Landers was wearing his everyday clothes"); the second is a noun

("Terashita comes to work every day"). The same applies to *everybody, everyone,* and *everything.*

exegesis/eisegesis See **eisegesis/exegesis.**

except/accept See **accept/except.**

exercise/exorcise To *exercise* requires physical exertion, the application of mental powers, or the using of one's rights. It can also refer to an act of worship, as in "religious exercises." To *exorcise* means to drive out an evil force by prayer or to free someone or something of evil spirits. It is possible to exorcise one's demons through exercise.

expect/anticipate See **anticipate/expect.**

explicate Use *explain* instead.

expurgated/unabridged/abridged See **abridged/expurgated/unabridged.**

extended family/nuclear family/tribe/clan See **clan/extended family/nuclear family/tribe.**

extrovert Not *extra-.*

fable/legend/myth/parable/allegory See **allegory/fable/legend/myth/parable.**

fact Only things directly capable of verification can properly be called facts. Do not use this word in matters of judgment.

fad words It is always best to avoid trendy language and vogue words or expressions. Also avoid jargon words that are unclear to outsiders. See **cant/jargon, clichés.**

faithful/fateful When an event or its outcome is *fateful,* it was (and is) controlled by fate or foreordained; *faithful* has to do with being loyal, dependable, and in good standing.

fanatic/zealot A *fanatic* is one who, out of overzealousness, goes to any length to practice or uphold his or her beliefs. A *zealot* is a person who is extremely devoted to a cause and is active in its support.

farrago/virago *Farrago* refers to a mixture of ideas or words that usually incorporate both fact and fantasy ("His testimony under oath was a farrago of truths, half-truths, exaggerations, and lies"). *Virago* means a loud, domineering, masculine woman.

farther/further *Farther* is usually used when speaking of literal distance ("Deerfield is farther from Chicago than Wheaton"). *Further* can be used in contexts involving figurative distance ("I can ride this train no further") and also in the sense of additional (as in *further details*).

fate/fete *Fate* is destiny. A *fete* is a festive occasion.

fateful/faithful See **faithful/fateful**.

fete/fate See **fate/fete**.

fewer/less *Fewer* refers to *a number of individual things. Less* refers to a *quantity or amount of one thing.* Use *fewer* if the word it modifies is plural. Use *less* if the word it modifies is singular. (Because of automation, *fewer* workers are needed. *Less* rain has fallen this season than was predicted.)

finalize Associated mostly with bureaucracy and big business. Better to avoid this pompous, ugly, and ambiguous verb. Try complete, conclude, finish, make final, or sum up.

fiscal/physical *Fiscal* relates to financial matters or to the public revenues, especially from taxation. *Physical* relates to the body (rather than the mind, the soul, or the feelings) or to something that can be touched or seen.

fission/fusion Both are ways of producing nuclear energy, the former by splitting the nucleus of an atom, and the latter by fusing two light nuclei into a single, heavier nucleus.

flaunt/flout The first means to display proudly or ostentatiously; the second means to defy. "Writers and editors flaunt their ignorance if they flout sound usage advice."

flotsam and jetsam *Flotsam* is floating debris, the wreckage of a ship and it goods. *Jetsam* describes the part of a ship and its cargo that is thrown overboard to lighten the load in times of distress. In olden times, while the flotsam was claimed by the king or government monarch, the jetsam belonged to the lord of the manor on whose land it washed up. Another term, *lagan* (but also spelled *lagend, lagon, ligan, ligen,* and *logan*), is like jetsam, except that a buoy is fastened to it for future location and recovery. In common usage, *flotsam and jetsam* usually appear together to mean debris.

forebade Preferred over *forbad.* The past tense of forbid.

forego/forgo *Forego* means to precede, but *forgo* means to do without.

for ever/forever The former is preferred and can mean either constantly or for all time.

forth/fourth Going forward or onward is to go *forth. Fourth* means after three others.

founder/flounder To *founder* means to collapse or break down suddenly. To *flounder* (probably a blend of founder and blunder) means to move clumsily or awkwardly in confusion. "The ship floundered aimlessly in the icy waters, and when it ran out of steam, it began to founder and go down." A *flounder* (noun) is also a type of ocean fish.

from . . . to The *from . . . to* construction denotes a logical progression. If you begin such a construction with *from* and end it with *to,* be sure to put in what goes between ("It is a joy to watch our children advance from toddlerhood to adolescence to adulthood"). If you really mean to say *as diverse as,* then say so ("We publish books as diverse as Bible commentaries, youth novels, and biographies").

fulsome *Fulsome* means excessive, disgusting, and revolting; *not* lavish, copius, plentiful or bountiful.

further/farther See **farther/further**.

fusion/fission See **fission/fusion**.

future plans Redundant. Use "plans" alone.

gage/gauge The first meaning of *gage* is as a symbol of a challenge to fight (such as a glove thrown to the ground). It also refers to a standard measure or measuring device. This latter meaning matches the definition of *gauge* (not *guage*), which also means to measure exactly or to form a judgment of something.

gender/sex *Sex* divides male and female (persons, animals, plants) and also refers to the character of being male or female. Originally, *gender* was strictly a grammatical term, but it became a way of referring to maleness or femaleness without using the word *sex.* Better to avoid the word *gender* if one can, for it is disdained by most authorities. See **manliness/manness/womanliness/womanness**.

genus/species The first is a subgroup of the second. People are of the genus *Homo* and the species *sapiens.*

gorilla/guerrilla A *gorilla* is an ape. A *guerrilla* (with two r's) is a secret warrior.

grisly/gristly/grizzly *Grisly* means horrifying. *Gristly* means full of gristle. *Grizzly* means gray-haired and also refers to a type of bear.

guarded condition This is a meaningless expression. A prognosis can be guarded but not a condition.

gynecocentric/androcentric See **androcentric/gyne-cocentric**.

hail/hale The first describes a greeting. The second means robust and healthy.

hanged/hung People are *hanged*, but objects are *hung*.

harass/harassment Not *harass/harassment*.

Hebrew/Yiddish These words are not interchangeable. *Hebrew* is a Semitic language. *Yiddish* (short for *yidish daytsh*, literally "Jewish German") is a Middle High German language written in Hebrew characters and spoken by Jews from central and eastern Europe (and also spoken by their descendants). See **Jew/Jewish/Judaism**.

hedonism Hedonists believe that happiness is the goal of life. But there are different varieties of hedonists: *egoistic hedonism* says that the goal of life is one's own happiness; *epicurism* (or *epicureanism*) says the goal of life is sensual gratification, as derived from food, drink, and easy living; *eudaemonism* says the goal of life is happiness and well-being attained through reason; *universalistic hedonism* posits the goal of life as the greatest happiness of the greatest number of people—that is, the interests and well-being of the multitude are more important that those of the individual.

heritage/legacy/lineage *Heritage* consists of the stories, memories, sayings, and personalities that make up the character of a generation, passed from one generation to the next. *Legacy* is a bequest or gift and can refer to an ancestor or predecessor passing on something tangible or intangible. *Lineage* has to do with names and dates.

High Church/Low Church Both terms are used in connection with the Anglican Church, or the Church of England. *High Church* refers to a conservative party that retains various practices and much of the liturgy of the Roman Catholic Church. *Low Church* applies to a more evangelical party that attaches relatively little importance to traditional Roman Catholic rituals.

Hindi/Hindu/Hindustani *Hindi* is the main language of India. A *Hindu* is a follower of Hinduism, the main religion of India. *Hindustani* is the main dialect of Western Hindi used in India.

historic/historical While *historic* refers to something renowned or history making, *historical* refers to things concerned with or contained in history.

HIV/AIDS Not *H.I.V.* See **AIDS/HIV**.

hoard/horde A *hoard* is a hiding place or cache. A *horde* is a swarm of people.

homograph/homonym/homophone *Homographs* are two or more words that are spelled alike but are different in pronunciation, meaning, or derivation (e.g., *plant* as a meaning for "to sow" and *plant* as another word for "factory"). *Homonyms* are two words that are spelled and pronounced alike but have two different meanings (e.g., *grate,* "fireplace" and *grate,* "to rub"). *Homophones* are words pronounced the same way, but they have a different spelling, meaning, or derivation (e.g., *bare* and *bear*).

hopefully Avoid using *hopefully* when you mean *it is to be hoped* or *we hope,* such as in this incorrect usage: "Hopefully, Christmas will soon be upon us." It is not Christmas that is doing the hoping.

horde/hoard See **hoard/horde**.

however When *however* is used in the sense of "in whatever way" or "to whatever extent," it can begin a sentence. ("However one arrives in Cheyenne, there are no shortcuts.") But it is best not to begin a sentence with *however* when using it to mean "nevertheless." ("The roads to Cheyenne were nearly impassable. At last, however, we arrived.")

hubris/sophrosyne *Hubris* is such great self-confidence that it can amount to arrogance. *Sophrosyne* is almost the opposite; it refers to temperance, modesty, prudence, and self-control.

hung/hanged See **hanged/hung**.

hurricane/tornado/tsunami/whirlwind/cyclone See **cyclone/hurricane/tornado/tsunami/whirlwind**.

ibid./op. cit. "In the work cited"; "in the same place." In references, Roman type should be used for Latin words and abbreviations (Ibid., et al., op cit., inter alia, and idem), except for [*sic*], which needs to appear distinct from quoted matter in which it appears (and usually is enclosed in brackets as shown here). In most cases, Latin abbreviations are not capitalized, with the exception of *Ibid.,* which usually appears at the beginning of a reference note.

idle/idol/idyll *Idle* means not working; an *idol* is an object of worship; *idyll* refers to an attractive scene or relationship.

i.e./e.g. See **e.g./i.e.**

illuminati Always plural.

immoral/amoral See **amoral/immoral**.

imply/infer/insinuate *Imply* means to intimate, to signify, or to hint. Imply means one is suggesting something without actually saying it. *Infer* means to deduce or to draw an inference or conclusion from evidence. Speakers *imply* things, whereas listeners *infer.* Insinuate describes an action not explicitly stated. Unlike the neutral *imply, insinuate* always has pejorative connotations.

impracticable/impractical *Impracticable* means that something cannot be done. *Impractical* and also *unpractical*) suggests that while something can probably be done, it is not worth doing.

in regard to This means the same as *as regards,* but it should not be written as *in regards to.*

in terms of Try less ponderous words, such as *about, as for, as to, concerning, for, regarding, respecting, through,* or *with.*

inchoate The word means incipient, just beginning, undeveloped. It does *not* mean disorganized or disorderly (it is sometimes misused in this way, probably because of its similarity in spelling to *chaotic*).

incomplete sentences In fiction you may use these for effect or in dialogue. For nonfiction, however, use incomplete sentences sparingly.

incunabula Books printed before 1500 AD.

indiscreet/indiscrete The former means lacking discretion, discernment, or prudence; the latter refers to something not individually distinct or something not composed of separate parts.

infectious/contagious See **contagious/infectious**.

infer/imply/insinuate See **imply/infer/insinuate**.

ingenious/ingenuous *Ingenious* means to be inventive or clever. *Ingenuous* means to be unsophisticated or innocent or open-minded.

ingest/egest See **egest/ingest**.

input Use only in its technical sense. Outside of computers, use more human terms. Try "we sought a stronger voice," or "we wanted a greater say," rather than "we wanted more input." See **chapter 9, "Publishing and Technology Helps," Section B, "Word Processing Terms."**

inquiry/enquiry See **enquiry/inquiry**.

insidious/invidious *Insidious* means either waiting for a chance to entrap or having an undesirable gradual and cumulative effect on something. *Invidious* means likely to cause offense, discontent, or envy.

insinuate/imply/infer See **imply/infer/insinuate**.

interface A technical word from science and engineering that should not be applied to human relations. Doctors and nurses should not *interface* more, but they probably should *work together* more effectively.

Internet, the Capitalize this word. See **chapter 9, "Publishing and Technology Helps," Section D, "Electronic Media Terms."**

intransitive verbs Intransitive verbs can express themselves without requiring a complement to complete their meaning. They therefore require no direct object. "The Grand Pooh-bah blushed." See **transitive verbs**.

irregardless/disregardless See **disregardless/irregardless**.

irritate/aggravate See **aggravate/irritate**.

Islam Islam is the religion of Muslims, not Mohammadism or Muhammadanism.

isle/aisle See **aisle/isle**.

it Avoid more than one use of the word *it* in a sentence unless the context makes perfectly clear who or what each *it* refers to.

its/it's *It's* is the contraction of *it is*; *its* is the possessive of "it."

jargon All jargon is pretentious and vacuous if not used very carefully. See **cant/jargon**.

jargon/cant See **cant/jargon**.

jealous/zealous One who is *jealous* feels suspicion or resentment due to rivalry or competition of some sort: "Lawrence is jealous of his younger brother." One who is *zealous* is active, devoted, and diligent: "Courtney is the most zealous worker in the church."

Jehovah's Witness, Witnesses Member(s) of the group known officially as the Watchtower Bible and Tract Society.

Jew/Jewish/Judaism A *Jew* is a believer in *Judaism* or a member of a Semitic people descended from the Hebrews, who existed in Palestine from the sixth century BC and who are now widely dispersed around the world. The adjective *Jewish* relates to one who practices Judaism or one who belongs to the race of Jews descended from the ancient Hebrews. *Jew, Jews, Jewish,* and *Jewishness* should never be used in a derogatory way (as in "Jewboy") or with either negative or positive connotations (negative: "Jew down" when talking about bargaining; positive: any well-to-do person, regardless of race or religion).

Jewess Do not use.

kibitz/kibbutz To *kibitz* is to offer advice that is not sought or wanted. It also has to do with watching or commenting upon a card game. A *kibbutz* is a communal settlement in Israel.

kind/kinds Make sure *kind* and its antecedent and *kinds* and its antecedent agree: "This kind . . ."; "These kinds . . ."

knave/nave A *knave* is a roguish man; a *nave* refers to both the main part of a church interior and a wheel hub.

Koran See **Qur'an or Qu'ran**, which are preferable. As an adjective, "koranic" without capitalization.

Latin Church/Western Church The term *Latin Church* refers to the liturgy and other rites of the Catholic Church as authorized by Rome. The term *Western Church* refers to the part of the Catholic Church that recognizes the pope, as well to all Christian churches of Western Europe and America.

law/statute *Law* suggests something laid down or settled, a body of rules of action or conduct enforced by a controlling authority. A *statute*, or *act*, is a formal, written expression of the law by a legislative body.

lay/lie *Lay* is a transitive verb ("I lay the book on the table") and should not be confused with *lie*, an intransitive verb ("I need to lie down"). The book was lying (not laying) on the table. Lay: lay (present), laid (past), have laid (present perfect); Lie: lie (present), lay (past), have lain (present perfect).

lead/led *Lead* is pronounced "led" only when it applies to metals. *Led* is the past tense and the past perfect tense of the verb *to lead*.

leave/let *Leave alone* if meaning "leaving someone in solitude"; *let alone* if meaning "refraining from interfering with."

legacy/lineage/heritage See **heritage/legacy/lineage**.

legend/myth/parable/allegory/fable See **allegory/fable/ legend/myth/parable**.

legendary Do not use this in the hype mode, as in "Max Perkins was a legendary editor." A *legend* is a tradition or story handed down from earlier times that is now popularly accepted as true or believable. But whereas a legend is a myth, Max Perkins was no myth.

lend/loan The former is a noun; the latter, a verb. "It is a good man whom you favor with a loan." "Friendship lasts if not asked to lend money."

less/fewer See **fewer/less**.

libel/plagiarism/scandal/slander While *libel* and *slander* both apply to false and defamatory statements about a living person (they both mean "defamation" or "injury to the reputation of someone"), the terms are not interchangeable. *Slander* applies to actual word of mouth. It is an oral defamation, spoken in the presence of a third person, that is false, malicious, and harmful but not put into print or any other graphic form. *Libel* applies to other such statements, whether written or printed words, pictures, signs, cartoons, broadcasts of television or radio, or any form other than speech, that expose a person to public hatred, shame, disgrace, or ridicule or that induce an ill opinion of the person. *Scandal* is malicious gossip or defamatory talk. It is a milder term than either libel or slander in that it is rumor and therefore suggests that whatever charges there are may be true or false. *Plagiarism* is an act of literary theft when using another's ideas or writings as one's own. It is presenting an idea as new and original when it was derived from an existing source.

license/licence In American usage, *license* is preferred for both noun and verb. (In British usage, *licence* is the noun and *license* is the verb.) With the exception of the word *practice,* however, the distinction in U.S. usage is also preserved for *device/devise, advice/advise,* and *prophecy/prophesy.*

lie/lay See **lay/lie.**

lifestyle Overly trendy, so use sparingly. Try simply "life" or "way of living."

like/as *Like* as a preposition is well established ("He writes like C. S. Lewis"). *Like* as a conjunction is widely prevalent but is not considered literate by most authorities and should still be avoided in formal writing. "C. S. Lewis writes like a good writer should" ought to be "C. S. Lewis writes as a good writer should." *Like* governs nouns and pronouns, but *as* should be used before phrases and clauses.

like/such as The basic idea of *like* is the similarity of one thing to some other thing. The basic idea of *such as* is the *identity* of one thing to some other thing.

lineage/legacy/heritage See **heritage/legacy/lineage.**

litany/liturgy A *litany* is a ceremonial form of prayer. *Liturgy* refers to public worship or a ritual of services.

literally Do not use *literally* when you mean *metaphorically;* it's the exact opposite. *Literally* means something that happened exactly as described. "Kim literally destroyed him with a look." Probably not, unless her look put him out of existence.

literati Not *litterati*.

liturgy/litany See **litany/liturgy**.

loan/lend See **lend/loan**.

logical fallacies and flaws in reasoning Watch out for these: *Argumentum ad hominem* literally means "argument against the man." Instead of talking about the point at issue, one attacks an opponent; an *argumentum ad captandum* is an "argument for pleasing"—pleasing the crowd by playing to their emotions. An *argumentum ad ignorantiam* says that something is true because no one has proved it untrue. An *indefinite proposition* refers to a group generalization, as in "all generalizations are false." An *exclusive proposition* is a more specific but also a hasty and untrue generalization, such as "only my son could get himself into this much trouble." A *formal fallacy* is one where the logical processes are wrong. An example of this would be "All dogs are loyal, and all cats are loyal. Therefore, all dogs are cats." A *material fallacy* involves distorting an issue. A *verbal fallacy* uses words improperly or ambiguously. A *fallacy of accident* treats something accidental or coincidental as if it were essential. An example of this would be, "The mouse caught in the trap was trying to eat the cheese, so obviously the cheese killed the mouse." The *fallacy of composition* says that what is true of one is true of all others in the group. The *fallacy of division* assumes that what is true of a group is also true of each individual member. The most common of all fallacies is the *either . . . or* fallacy, which says we have to choose between A or B, even when other choices are possible.

logology This word denotes the study of words.

lostness Obviously, the condition of being lost. This should, however, be used more often in a psychological and theological sense than a geographical one. "The current decade is one of lostness for most Americans."

Low Church/High Church See **High Church/Low Church**.

magnum opus/opus magnum A *magnum opus* is an author's masterpiece or principal work. An *opus magnum* is a great work. Do not italicize.

maleficence/malfeasance/misfeasance/nonfeasance
Malfeasance is clear wrongdoing. *Misfeasance* is performing a legal act illegally or improperly. *Nonfeasance* is failure to act or do what clearly needs to be done. Another word, *maleficence* (formed from malefic), is not a legal term, as are the first three; it means hurtful or harmful.

mandatary/mandatory *Mandatory* means obligatory or compulsory, whereas *mandatary* refers to one holding a mandate or authority to perform a certain task.

manliness/manness/womanliness/womanness
Manness and *womanness* refer to the distinctive features or essence of being a man or a woman. *Manliness* and *womanliness* refer more to appearance and superficial actions. See **sex/gender**.

mantel/mantle A shelf over a fireplace is a *mantel*. A cloak or cover is a *mantle*.

mean/median *Mean* means unkind, cruel, of low socal position, nongenerous, and base. It also means of intermediate or average value. *Median* means middle point. In the sequence 3 4 5 9 9, the median is 5; the average or mean is 6 (30÷5); the *mode* (or item appearing most frequently in the series) is 9.

media/medium *Media* is plural (television and newspapers are media); *medium* is singular (television is a medium). In addition, *medium* is the correct word to describe a person who claims to be a channel to the spirit world.

meet/mete *Meet* means suitable or proper. A fitting punishment, thus, is meet. Also, the idea behind "help-meet" is a correct or proper mate. The word also means to come face-to-face with. *Mete* means to distribute or allot (as in when one metes out punishment).

metaphor/simile While allied in meaning, a *simile* expresses resemblance directly with "as," "as if," and "like" ("She is clever like a fox"), but a *metaphor* is a fig-ure of speech where a term or phrase is applied to some-thing to which it is not literally applicable ("She is a fox").

militate/mitigate The first means to have weight or effect or to serve as a strong influence ("The facts mili-tated against us"). The second means to make less intense or serious, to soften, alleviate, or mollify (as in "mitigat-ing circumstances").

minister/pastor/priest A clergyman or clergywoman may go by many titles: pastor, minister, priest, rabbi, preacher, parson, cleric, reverend, and others. *Pastor* means "shepherd" and is used of one who has the spiri-tual care of people entrusted to his charge. *Minister* means "servant" and is a general term suggesting one who serves the spiritual needs of others. *Priest* refers to one who per-forms religious rites and is a title used mostly by Roman Catholic, Anglican (Episcopal), and Eastern Orthodox clergy. See **reverence/reverend/reverent**.

misfeasance/nonfeasance/maleficence/malfeasance See **maleficence/malfeasance/misfeasance/nonfeasance**.

misogamist/misogynist A *misogamist* (pronounced with a hard *g* sound) hates marriage. A *misogynist* (pronounced with a *j* sound) hates women.

Mohammed See **Muhammad**.

morality/ethics See **ethics/morality**.

more than/over There is no good reason *over* can't be used for *more than*.

Mormon Church Officially, the Church of Jesus Christ of Latter-Day Saints.

Moslem See **Muslim**.

Muhammad Preferred over Mohammed.

Muslim This is the preferred spelling for a follower of Muhammad (not Mohammed) or an adherent of Islam.

myth/parable/allegory/fable/legend See **allegory/fable/legend/myth/parable**.

naked/nude Both mean without clothing. *Naked* connotes vulnerablity, loss of dignity, or figuratively bare. *Nude* is usually used in reference to art.

Native American Preferred over Indian or American Indian when speaking of the original inhabitants of America.

naught/nought *Naught* means nothing, as in "Gail's work came to naught." *Nought* represents the figure zero. See **aught/ought**.

naval/navel *Naval* has to do with ships; *navels* are belly buttons.

nave/knave See **knave/nave**.

nephalist/teetotaler The story is that *teetotaler* originated with a nondrinker who stuttered "I'm a t-t-total abstainer." A *nephalist* (from the Greek, meaning "to drink no wine") is one who totally abstains from alcoholic drinks. *Nephalist* is a more formal word for *teetotaler.*

nevertheless One word, same as *nonetheless.*

nobody One word, but **no one**.

none Usually goes best with a singular verb.

nonfeasance/maleficence/malfeasance/misfeasance See **maleficence/malfeasance/misfeasance/nonfeasance**.

nonsexist use of language Women should receive the same treatment as men in all areas of writing. Physical descriptions, sexist references, demeaning stereotypes, and condescending phrases should not be used. References to humanity in general should use language that includes women. Instead of always using words such as *man* or *mankind,* attempt to use words such as *people, persons,* or *humanity.* The use of *he* as the pronoun for nouns embracing both genders has been the accepted usage for centuries. Inserting *he or she* or *his or her* is not the solution. "An editor must maintain good rapport with his or her authors," is obviously awkward. If possible, revise the sentence. For example, "Editors must maintain good rapport with their authors." The lack of a common-gender pronoun in English has led to some interesting experimental monstrosities, such as "heshe" for he or she, "s/he" for she or he, "himer" for him or her, "hiser" for his or her, and "himerself" for himself or herself. Of course, these would sound too strange to be used in speech, and as they deviate so dramatically from normal language, they should not be used in formal writing.

normalcy Not universally accepted. Use *normality* instead.

not hardly This is a double negative and is substandard. Use *hardly.*

notwithstanding One word.

nought/naught See **naught/nought**.

nouns into verbs Turning nouns into verbs can be handy: to telephone, to cable, to bus. But do not use noun-spawned verbs that serve no real purpose. For example, John is the author of seven books; he has not authored seven books.

nuclear family/tribe/clan/extended family See **clan/ extended family/nuclear family/tribe**.

numismatics The study and collection of coins or medals.

o/oh/oho *O* usually appears in religious contexts and is always capitalized. *Oh* is used in general contexts to show emotion and is not capitalized except at the beginning of a sentence. *Oho* shows surprise and can be used with or without an exclamation mark.

off of Redundant.

OK/okay May be written with or without periods, or as *okay*. Though overused, as a noun and verb it is acceptable for informal writing; but avoid its use as an adjective and adverb.

on the cutting edge An overworked and therefore moribund phrase.

one another/each other See **each other/one another**.

op. cit./ibid. See **ibid./op. cit.**

opposite/reverse/contrary/converse See **contrary/ converse/opposite/reverse**.

option Don't overuse. You have an option to use the word *choice*.

opus magnum/magnum opus See **magnum opus/opus magnum**.

or/and See **and/or**.

oral/aural See **aural/oral**.

oral/verbal *Verbal* refers to words of any kind, including things expressed in writing; *oral* refers to spoken words contrasted with written ones.

ordinal numbers/cardinal numbers See **cardinal numbers/ordinal numbers**.

ordinance/ordnance An *ordinance* is a decree or enactment. *Ordnance* (plural) are military supplies.

ostensibly This does *not* mean demonstrably true or real. It means that something is plausible or seemingly reasonable to outward appearances.

ought/aught See **aught/ought**.

over/more than See **more than/over**.

paean/paeon/peon A *paean* is a song of praise. *Paeon* refers to a metrical foot in ancient Greek and Latin poetry. *Peon* means peasant or a servant.

pail/pale A *pail* is a small bucket. *Pale* means lacking color; it can also mean a real or metaphorical boundary.

palate/palette/pallet The *palate* is the roof of the mouth. A *palette* is a thin board on which an artist mixes colors for painting. A *pallet* is a makeshift bed and also a large tray or platform used for lifting or storage.

pandemic/endemic/epidemic See **endemic/epidemic/pandemic**.

parable/allegory/fable/legend/myth See **allegory/fable/legend/myth/parable**.

partially/partly While *partly* means in part (as distinct from the whole) and *partially* means incompletely or to a certain degree, it is usually true that fine-drawn distinctions between these two words are not very useful.

passable/passible The former means capable of being passed ("The road was passable") or barely satisfactory ("The food was passable"); the latter means capable of feeling or suffering.

pastor/priest/minister See **minister/pastor/priest**.

peak/peek A *peak* is a summit; *peek* means to steal a look.

penniless Not *pennyless*.

peon/paean/paeon See **paean/paeon/peon**.

percent, percentage One word.

percept/precept A *percept* is an impression of something perceived. A *precept* is a rule or principle that guides somebody's actions or moral behavior.

persecute/prosecute The former is to harass or to cause to suffer. The latter is to bring legal proceedings against someone or to take to court.

personalize(d) Pretentious. As an adjective, use *personal* instead.

persuade/convince See **convince/persuade**.

pidgin/creole See **creole/pidgin**.

pity/sympathy/commiseration/compassion/empathy See **commiseration/compassion/empathy/pity/sympathy**.

plagiarism See **libel/plagiarism/scandal/slander**.

plus A word from mathematics that can be an *occasional* replacement for also, moreover, not only that, and but. But never begin a sentence with *plus*.

PM/AM or p.m./a.m. See **AM/PM or a.m./p.m.**

poetry/verse When fewer than four lines of poetry or verse are quoted, set in Roman type and enclose in quotation marks within the same paragraph. Separate each line of poetry or verse with a slash (solidus, diagonal), and a thin but equal amount of space on either side:

"Build thee more stately mansions, oh my soul, / While the swift seasons roll." When four or more lines are quoted, omit the quotation marks and center the entire block on the longest line. If the lines are longer than the column width in which they are to be set, indent the beginning of each new line one em space instead, and bring the remainder of the line out to the left margin.

pore/pour To *pore* means to examine something carefully, as when one pores over a book. *Pour* (noun) is also a small opening in the skin. *Pour* refers to an action of pouring or a heavy downfall of rain.

poser/poseur A *poser* is a puzzle, but a *poseur* is an insincere person or a person of affected manner.

practicable/practical Both mean able to be done. When a thing can be done and is worth doing, it is *practical*. When a thing can be done, whether or not it is worth doing, it is *practicable*.

practical/pragmatic The word *pragmatic* comes from the field of philosophy and means the intellectual acceptance of whatever is workable as true or sound. ("Diana took a pragmatic approach to the problem.") *Practical* involves activity as distinct from study or theory. ("Living abroad can be a very practical experience.")

practically/virtually *Virtually* means almost or in effect. *Practically* means in practice or to all practical purposes. Do not use *practically* when you mean almost. Otherwise, these words are *virtually/practically* interchangeable.

practice/practise In American usage, *practice* is preferred for both noun and verb. (In British usage, *practice* is the noun and *practise* is the verb.) With the exception of the word *license,* however, the distinction in U.S. usage is preserved for *device/devise, advice/advise,* and *prophecy/prophesy.*

pragmatic/practical See **practical/pragmatic**.

pre- Be careful with this prefix. *Pre-* does not always add to the sense of words where it is affixed and can often be removed. Examples: precondition, preperformance, preplanning, and prescreen.

precipitant/precipitate/precipitous *Precipitant* and *precipitate* are close in meaning: a headlong rush. But where the first indicates the abruptness of the rush, the second emphasizes the rashness of it. *Precipitous* means like a precipice, or steep.

prepositions at end of sentences The prohibition regarding using prepositions at the end of sentences is an affectation, and for most authorities the "rule" has been discarded. There are many sentences where the preposition could scarcely come anywhere else, as in "This bed hasn't been slept in." On ending sentences with a preposition, C. S. Lewis has said that "the silly 'rule' against it was invented by Dryden. I think he disliked it only because you can't do it in either French or Latin which he thought more 'polite' languages than English."

prescribe/proscribe *Prescribe* means to order or to instruct, as in a doctor prescribing medicine. *Proscribe* means to forbid or denounce, as in a doctor proscribing smoking.

presently This adverb means "in a short while." It should not be used for "currently."

principal/principle *Principal* can be a noun meaning chief or of first importance ("Matt is the principal of the school"), or an adjective with the same meaning ("My principal reason for writing the book is . . ."). *Principle* is a noun and means fundamental ("It's the principle of the thing").

prize/reward *Prize* refers to something won in competition, overt or otherwise. A *reward* conveys the idea of recompense both for wrongdoing and for good.

prone/prostrate/supine All mean "lying flat" or "level with the ground." But the literal meaning of *prostrate* is "reduced to weakness" and "helpless"—lying either face down or face up in submission or for protection. Technically, *prone* refers to a face-down position, and *supine* to a face-up position.

prophecy/prophesy The former, a prediction or revelation of what is to come, is a noun. The latter means "to predict" or "to foretell" and is a verb. "I prophesy the dissolution of communism; that is my prophecy."

proscribe/prescribe See **prescribe/proscribe**.

prosecute/persecute See **persecute/prosecute**.

prostrate/prone/supine See **prone/prostrate/supine**.

pseudonym/cryptonym See **cryptonym/pseudonym**.

purple passages These occur when a writer inserts into uncolorful and commonplace writing something that is conspicuous for brilliance or effectiveness (commonly named a *purple passage* or *purple patch*). This obtrusively ornate, flowery prose is looked on disparagingly because of the unevenness of such writing. Such passages should be avoided. One should also avoid **bathos**, the converse of purple passages: the sudden appearance of the commonplace in otherwise elevated matter or style.

purposefully/purposely *Purposely* means doing something on purpose, or with an intended result.

Purposefully means having a particular purpose or objective in mind.

Pyrrhic victory/Cadmean victory See **Cadmean victory/Pyrrhic victory**.

query/inquiry/enquiry A *query* is a single question. This is also true of an *inquiry* (or *enquiry*), but an inquiry can also apply to a more extensive investigation. In the United States, *inquiry* and *inquire* are preferred over *enquiry* and *enquire*.

Qur'an or Qu'ran These are now considered the more accurate contemporary spellings instead of *Koran* (just as *Beijing* is now accepted instead of *Peking*).

rack/wrack The former means to put under strain, as in "nerve-racking"; the latter means to wreck, and it usually appears in the redundant expression "wrack and ruin."

radical From the Latin *radix,* meaning root or proceeding from a root. *Radical* relates to the origin or the fundamentals of a thing, and in its precise sense means someone wanting to get to the root of a matter. It has, however, taken on the meaning of drastic reform (especially as regards leftist or revolutionary causes) and a complete departure from established customs. The word should not be used in a Humpty-Dumpty fashion to refer to those with whom we disagree. Unfortunately, there is no neutral word for those who want fundamental change.

raise/raze To *raise* means to cause or help to rise to a standing position. To *raze* means to reduce to ground level. It is superfluous to say that a building is "razed to the ground."

rational/rationale *Rational* means of sound mind; *rationale* is an underlying basis or reason for something.

ravage/ravish To lay waste or to devastate is to *ravage.* To rape or carry off is to *ravish,* but this word also has the sense of filling with delight.

raze/raise See **raise/raze**.

re- words Use a hyphen to distinguish between a one-word form and a compound with a different meaning: recollect (remember), but re-collect (collect again); recede (withdraw), but re-cede (to give back again).

reason why If *reason* is used as a noun, it should never be followed by *why.* ("The reason I'm suggesting this is . . .") But if the tone is conversational, sometimes *why* may be used. ("Lisa sees no reason why we should not publish this book.")

rebut/refute *Refute* renders a verdict and means to disprove evidence or an accusation, or to demolish in an argument. *Rebut* also means to disprove, but it is somewhat more neutral when it means reply to, deny, contend, and contradict.

refer back/revert back Both are redundant—*back* is not needed.

registered brand names See **trademarks**.

regretfully/regrettably *Regretfully* is with feelings of regret; *regrettably* means unfortunately.

relate(s) to Outside of the social sciences, this is a vague term.

religious terminology Clubby, insular, phrases such as "The Lord laid it on my heart," "look to the Lord in prayer," and "prayer warrior" may have an unclear meaning to your readers. Keep in mind your audience and make sure they will understand exactly what you are talking about. Strive for clear, efficient, and thoughtful ways to say what you want to say.

replica An exact copy, not a scale model or miniature. A replica is something built to the same dimensions and using the same materials. (In art, however, a replica is a duplicate made by the original artist.)

replicate Use *repeat exactly* or *duplicate* instead.

reply/response/answer See **answer/reply/response**.

resupply Redundant. Use *supply*.

reverence/reverend/reverent *Reverence* is a noun for deference or adoration. Except for its official use as a title, *reverend* is used primarily as an adjective, meaning "deserving of respect, awe, love, or reverence." Avoid using it alone as a noun, for it is not correct to say, for example, "The reverend will be with you shortly." *Reverent* is an adjective that describes someone who displays reverence. See **minister/pastor/priest**.

reverse/contrary/converse/opposite See **contrary/converse/opposite/reverse**.

revert back/refer back See **refer back/revert back**.

reward/prize See **prize/reward**.

right/rite/wright/write *Right* as an adjective means correct, and as a noun, entitlement. A *rite* is a religious ceremony. *Wright* refers to a craftsman or craftswoman (e.g., a playwright). One puts pen to paper to *write*.

rob Peter to pay Paul A tired and ineffective metaphor.

saint Spell out in text. Abbreviate in parenthetical use, in addresses, in names of cities or persons and in any tabular use.

same difference A fusion of "same thing" and "no

difference." Acceptable but confusing and good to avoid.

scandal/slander/libel/plagiarism See **libel/plagiarism/scandal/slander**.

scared/scarred Being *scared* is being frightened. Being *scarred* is being disfigured.

scent/sent/cent See **cent/scent/sent**.

sealing/ceiling See **ceiling/sealing**.

secondly, thirdly, . . . The *-ly* is unnecessary. When someone writes (or says) a list, it should go like this: "I want to make three points: First, blah, blah, blah. Second, blah, blah, blah. Third, blah, blah, blah." Making the numbers into adverbs by adding "ly" in the subsequent references is grammatically incorrect. This is a common writing mistake, but it keeps editors in business.

seize/cease See **cease/seize**.

self-confessed Since no one can confess on another's behalf, just use *confessed.*

seminary A graduate divinity school for training ministers, priests, or rabbis. Sometimes also used for a school of secondary grade for young men and women.

sensual/sensuous *Sensual* is a less favorable term. It suggests worldly, irreligious sexuality and is equivalent to carnal or lewd. *Sensuous* does not have these connotations. It means pertaining to the senses.

service marks See **trademarks**.

set/sit The former is transitive, concerning an action people do to a thing, and needs an object to complete its meaning. It means "to put." The latter is intransitive and is something that people simply *do,* and it does not need an object. It means "to place oneself."

sex/gender See **gender/sex**.

sexism in language See **nonsexist use of language**.

shall/will In formal writing, the future tense requires *shall* for the first person, *will* for the second and third. To express the author's belief regarding future action or state is *I shall*; *I will* expresses the author's determination or consent. Today, however, the distinction *shall* and *will* has blurred, and generally either is accepted as proper usage.

shudder/shutter To *shudder* is to tremble, quiver, or shake. A *shutter* (noun) is a covering that controls the passage of light, usually movable, over a window, door, or camera lens. To *shutter* (verb) means to close or to furnish with shutters.

sic Latin: So; thus; as it was; in this way. It means something is used or spelled "in that way." *Sic* is inserted in brackets into a text to show a misspelling or an anomaly that has not been corrected in order to quote it exactly as it was given. Write it as [*sic*] in italics.

simile/metaphor See **metaphor/simile**.

sine qua non Latin for "without which not." Use only when you are meaning something that is absolutely essential. Do not capitalize or put into italics.

sit/set See **set/sit**.

site/cite See **cite/site**.

slander/libel/plagiarism/scandal See **libel/plagiarism/scandal/slander**.

slough When it rhymes with "cow" it means a swamp or marshy place and also a state of hopeless depression. But when it rhymes with "rough" it means to shed skin.

sober/somber *Sober* means showing no excessive or extreme qualities. It represents temperance, moderation, or seriousness. *Somber* means dark and gloomy, or of depressing character.

soluble/solvable A thing that is *soluble* can be dissolved. Something that is *solvable* can be solved.

sophrosyne/hubris See **hubris/sophrosyne**.

special/especial See **especial/special**.

species/genus See **genus/species**.

split infinitives An infinitive is "to" and a verb such as *to write, to edit, to play.* An infinitive functions in a sentence as a noun. The "rule" against splitting infinitives (putting an adverb between "to" and the verb, as in "I opened the door to forcibly eject him") once was an unbreakable one enforced by grammar teachers and editors with harsh punishment. Now, while splitting an infinitive still should be avoided most of the time, the split infinitive is not a grammatical error but is often a rhetorical fault. It is acceptable if it makes the sentence read better than any of the alternatives. Splitting an infinitive with the word *not,* however, still should be avoided. Shakespeare was correct: "To be or not to be. That is the question."

stanch/staunch The first means to stop the flowing of blood; the second means steadfast in loyalty.

strategy Better words are plan, scheme, design, or method.

stationary/stationery To be *stationary* means to stand still or not move. *Stationery* (a plural noun) is writing paper, envelopes, and other articles for correspondence.

statute/law See **law/statute**.

such as/like See **like/such as**.

Sunday School/Sunday school Do not capitalize *school* unless you are referring to a particular Sunday school. "He teaches a class at Walker Memorial Sunday School"; but: "He teaches Sunday school at Walker Memorial Church."

supersede Not *supercede*.

supine/prone/prostrate See **prone/prostrate/supine**.

supportive of Don't weaken the verb by turning it into an adjective with a preposition. Just say *supported*.

sympathy/commiseration/compassion/empathy/pity See **commiseration/compassion/empathy/pity/sympathy**.

take/bring See **bring/take**.

team/teem A *team* is a group of people engaged in a united effort, but it can also apply to animals. *Teem* means to flow and overflow.

teenager Although still hyphenated in some dictionaries, it's more common usage is as one word.

teetotaler/nephalist See **nephalist/teetotaler**.

that/which *That* is a defining, or restrictive, pronoun, and *which* is a nondefining, or nonrestrictive, pronoun. "The copy machine that is broken is down the hall" tells which one. "The copy machine, which is broken, is down the hall" adds a fact about the copy machine in question. A way to check is to ask if the sentence needs commas. If so, insert the commas and leave *which*; if not, change *which* to *that*.

theater/theatre Both are correct, but *theater* is preferred by most (except by those in the theatrical professions).

thee/thine/thou Avoid the use of the Old English pronoun and verb forms except where used in direct quotations or for special effect.

this day and age A worn-out, dim-witted redundancy.

though/although See **although/though**.

thus Watch the context of this. The basic meaning

should be "in this manner" and "therefore." It should not be used when meaning "for example."

together with/along with See **along with/together with**.

tornado/tsunami/whirlwind/cyclone/hurricane See **cyclone/hurricane/tornado/tsunami/whirlwind**.

tortuosity/tortuous/torturous *Tortuosity* is crookedness, sinuousness, or deviousness. ("The tortuosity of his arguments angered us.") *Tortuous* means winding, twisting, and circuitous. It is also used figuratively in the sense of something complicated or convoluted, as in the tortuous language of the tax codes. *Torturous* has to do with a painful ordeal.

trademarks/service marks/registered brand names Please make every effort to find out if a specific term is a trademark, service mark, or brand name and always capitalize it as is dictated. Keep in mind that standard trademark protection is sometimes given to names used in published fiction, as well as to famous book titles. The general rule is to use a generic equivalent unless the trademark name is essential to the writing. In running text, one need not use the symbols that usually accompany registered trademark names on product packaging and advertising. Here are some examples:

> Anacin, Bufferin, Excedrin, Tylenol, etc. (but *aspirin*)
> Astroturf
> Bakelite (but *plastic resin*)
> Band-Aid
> CinemaScope
> Clorox (but *bleach*)
> Coca-Cola or Coke
> Dacron (but *polyester*)
> Formica

Frigidaire (but *refrigerator*)
Gone with the Wind
Jeep (for Chrysler cars, but *jeep* for army vehicles)
Jell-O (but *gelatin dessert*)
Kleenex (but *facial tissue*)
Kodak (but *camera*)
LifeWay
Levi's (but *blue denim jeans*)
Life Saver(s)
Muzak
Novocaine
Orlon (but *acrylic fiber*)
Scotch tape
Plexiglas
Styrofoam
Technicolor movies
Telephoto
TelePrompTer
Thermos
TruthQuest
Vaseline (but *petroleum jelly*)
Winnie the Pooh
Xerox (but *photocopier*)

transitive verbs Transitive verbs require a direct object because they cannot complete their meaning without the help of a complement. "Pam sent flowers." See **intransitive verbs**.

translate/transliterate These words are not interchangeable. *Translate* means to turn text or words into one's own or another language or to express in more comprehensible terms. *Transliterate* means changing the characters or letters or other symbols of one language into those used in another.

transpire From the Latin, "breathe through." *Transpire* should be used in the sense of "become known" or "to leak through." ("The truth of the mystery finally transpired.") It should not be use for "to happen" or "to come to pass."

tribe/clan/extended family/nuclear family See **clan/extended family/nuclear family/tribe**.

trillion/billion See **billion/trillion**.

trivia Always plural.

troop/troupe A gathering of soldiers is a *troop*. A company of actors is a *troupe*.

trustee/trusty A *trustee* is a person responsible for business affairs or property. Someone who is *trusty* is a trusted person.

2004 *2004* is the correct way to indicate the year, not 2,004.

unabridged/abridged/expurgated See **abridged/expurgated/unabridged**.

unexceptionable/unexceptional The later means ordinary, not outstanding, or not remarkable; the former means not open to objections.

uninterested/disinterested See **disinterested/uninterested**.

unique One of a kind. Do not use *unique* with a modifier. It is impossible for a thing to be "more unique" or "one of the most unique."

university/college See **college/university**.

unman/unnerve/enervate/emasculate See **emasculate/enervate/unman/unnerve**.

usage/use Largely interchangeable, except that *usage* is better in contexts that involve languages ("contemporary English usage"). *Use*, however, is preferred in most other cases.

utilize Never use this for *use*. The strict meaning of *utilize* is to make use of something that wasn't intended for the job. "She utilized a paintbrush to apply her makeup." Outside of that strict meaning, always choose *use*.

venal/venial *Venal* means corruptible and describes someone capable of being bought. *Venial* means excusable, pardonable, or easily forgiven. A venial sin in the Roman Catholic Church, for example, is much less serious than a mortal sin.

venerate/worship In the religious context *worship* should apply only to God. Roman Catholics and others *worship* God but *venerate* saints.

verbal agreement This can mean either a written or a spoken agreement, so spell it out if the manner of agreeing is important. When the meaning is limited to what is transmitted by speech, use *oral agreement* to be precise.

verbal/oral See **oral/verbal**.

verse/poetry See **poetry/verse**.

viable When referring to ideas, this means practicable. When referring to plants and animals, it means capable of living.

viable alternative Used in the sense of a sound or workable alternative. But as we do not usually seek an unsound or unworkable alternative, the adjective is redundant and should be dropped.

virago/farrago See **farrago/virago**.

virtual *Virtual* does not mean "actual," and it does not mean "nearly." It means that something has the effect but not the form. "He is operating as the virtual head of the company until a new president is named."

virtually/practically See **practically/virtually**.

wail/wale/whale A *wail* is a mournful cry, while a *wale* is a streak or ridge; a *whale*, of course, is the underwater mammal.

waiver/waver A *waiver* is the abandoning of a claim or privilege. To *waver* means to vacillate or hesitate between choices.

wane/wax *Wax* means to grow gradually larger. *Wane* means the exact opposite.

was/were Alike in that they both form the past tense of the verb *be*. But the subjunctive mood, *were,* is used to express a condition of probability: a condition contrary to fact, a supposition, an improbable condition, an uncertainty or doubt, a necessity, or a desire. "I wish I were there" (desire). "Suppose she were to come over tomorrow" (supposition). "He ate as if food were going out of style" (improbable condition).

Web See **World Wide Web**.

weltanschauung German for *worldview.* Do not capitalize or italicize.

Western Church/Latin Church See **Latin Church/Western Church**.

whale/wail/wale See **wail/wale/whale**.

whence/wherein Both are somewhat archaic.

which/that See **that/which**.

White See **African American/black**.

who/whom/whose Use *who* and *whom* for references to human beings and to animals with a name. Use *that* and *which* for inanimate objects and animals without a name. *Whose* can be used in regard to both persons and things. ("I could a tale unfold whose lightest word / Would harrow up thy soul.") *Who* is used when someone is the subject of a sentence, clause, or phrase. ("The man who bought the book forgot it and left it on the counter." "Who is it?") *Whom* is used when someone is the object of a verb or preposition (i.e., "The man to whom the book was sold forgot and left it on the counter." "Whom do you wish to see?").

will/shall See **shall/will**.

womanliness/womanness/manliness/manness See **manliness/manness/womanliness/womanness**.

World Wide Web/Web/WWW Capitalize this phrase, but the word is *worldwide* (not world-wide) when used in a general sense. See **chapter 9, "Publishing and Technology Helps," Section D, "Electronic Media Terms."**

worldview Not *world view* or *world-view*.

worship/venerate See **venerate/worship**.

worshiped/worshiping American usage spells these words with a single *p*.

worst comes to worst Not *worse comes to worst* or *worse comes to worse*. This phrase is somewhat of a cliché—use sparingly.

wrack/rack See **rack/wrack**.

wright/write/right/rite See **right/rite/wright/write**.

WWW See **World Wide Web**.

xenophile/xenophobe A *xenophile* likes foreigners and foreign culture, but a *xenophobe* dislikes or fears these things.

Xmas Although *Xmas* has been used as a way to spell *Christmas* for centuries (the *X* represents Jesus Christ as well as the cross and the Greek letter *chi*), many think of this word as disrespectful and even sacrilegious, and it is not considered appropriate in formal writing.

Yiddish/Hebrew See **Hebrew/ Yiddish**.

zealot/fanatic See **fanatic/zealot**.

zealous/jealous See **jealous/zealous**.

CHAPTER 9
Publishing and Technology Helps

A. Suggestions on Choosing and Using Technology

"Electronic word processing" is the term used here for the work of computing in writing and publishing. The tools needed for a writer to do word processing are a computer or other system that provides a word-processing application, a keyboard, a screen, a printer, a set of disks to store the work—and a human mind. Put another way, no one *needs* a computer to write. All one *needs* is a fertile mind, a pen, and some paper. Typewriters were not used for writing before the 1870s, and until the 1970s computers were not used for this purpose, either. Writing can go on without computing, as it has for centuries. Even so, while high technology will not *make* you a writer, it will almost certainly save you an enormous amount of time and energy *in* your writing. It will enhance the creative process by making the mechanics of writing much easier.

Even a technophobe can learn to use a computer. One

need master no secret language to benefit from computers with word-processing software. With only a minor amount of fidgeting, writers can quickly surpass what they were capable of doing with manual, electric, and even electronic typewriters. One thing is sure: preparing manuscripts electronically is absolutely required for writing in the twenty-first century.

What can a computer do for you? It can function as an electronic file cabinet, but it can do much more. Its cut-and-paste and editing features can allow you to produce material without blemish and without having to retype the entire manuscript, letting you design and dress up your material. You can immediately see altered text clearly and without rekeyboarding. With an electronic writing system, you can easily and painlessly revise and reprint your work until you've got it the way you want it. With some computers you can create graphics and type layout for desktop publishing of everything from newsletters to full-length books. With a modem you can send your work directly from your computer to the computer of your publisher. You can do repetitive mechanical chores, such as filing and alphabetizing, in much less time. You can actually type faster, as fast as you can go, with words appearing instantly on the screen. Your manuscript can be printed much faster than anyone could type it, with mechanically perfect results. You can double or triple your writing production. All of these things, and many others, make computers wondrous machines. Most writers will agree that writing with the aid of word processing can be exciting and rewarding.

The benefits of working with computers in your writing will outweigh the few difficulties that you will encounter. For example, something to keep in mind when working with computers is that they can eat words alive. Disaster can occur in dozens of ways, including a sudden loss of electrical power, damage to the storage medium, and simple accidental erasure due to user error. You could be reaching across the keyboard for coffee and inadvertently hit some unknown combination of buttons, losing a whole day's work. Advice: Be a bit paranoid and hit the "save" key often. Storing backup copies of your computer disks is also a good idea. Be sure to handle disks properly to avoid damage. Pay close attention when editing, moving, or deleting parts of a document. Remember that these machines can only do exactly what we tell them, and they do it instantly and obediently. If and when a disastrous problem happens, it's almost always because we've given the wrong message. Usually word processors are reliable.

The work of the writer will never change, even with the focus on new technology. Writers still need to face an empty page (or an empty screen) and try to fill it up with good and original ideas. But working on a word processor can offer a new and valuable perspective on the writer's art. If you have not done so yet, you will want to consider how to choose a computer system.

First, learn what is available. Find a system you are comfortable with. Explore its capabilities. Learn to care for and feed your computer. Learn the mechanics of computer writing and editing, and master how you can produce elegant manuscripts. Remember to choose the hardware first (evaluate the keyboard, screen, and editing features), and then choose the best available software. Find a good laser printer, and make sure the word-processing program you want to use supports it. (Be careful of printers designed to run only with certain software programs.) Writers will want to make sure they work with a program that displays the formatted text on the screen during the writing and editing process. This shows you the spacing of words and lines and how the pages will look, giving you the results of your formatting choices while you are doing your writing.

B. Word Processing Terms

application A program or group of programs designed for the end user. Applications software includes database programs, spreadsheets, and word processors.

backup As a verb (*back up*), to copy files to a second storage medium such as a disk as a precaution in case the copy on the computer hard drive is lost or corrupted. As a noun, the file that has been copied is called a *backup*.

bold or boldface A darker form of the typeface and size that is being used as the standard for the document.

boot To begin a computer program or to ready one for use; also, to load a disk into the disk drive.

clipboard A place within the word-processing system in which you can temporarily put text that you are going to copy or paste into a document.

cursor An arrow, blinking box, blinking underline, or any character-sized indicator that can be used to move around a monitor screen, accomplishing a variety of tasks.

cut and paste To remove text or graphic from a place in a document and place it on the clipboard for positioning in another place within the document.

defaults Font styles, formatting, margin settings, and other "automatic" document characteristics that have been built into a word-processing system by the manufacturer; the user can override them or reset them if they are not appropriate to the document being processed.

disk (or disc) drive The storing device that holds the electronic text; it makes the magnetic disk (or **diskette**) spin in order to read the information on the disk and display it on the monitor.

editing (through the word-processing system)

Basic editing capabilities include an *overstrike* feature, in which errors can be corrected by simply typing over them on the screen, with the new letters taking the place of the old ones. *Insertions* and *deletions* are also basic: Characters, letters, words, phrases, paragraphs, pages, even whole documents can be inserted or deleted from the text instantly at your instruction. Electronic *cut and paste* (see definition) is another basic editing capability. *Column creation or moving, calculator capabilities, spell check,* and *pagination* capabilities are also usually basic to a software editing package.

Advanced editing features include *search and replace,* allowing you to substitute a string of text for another one throughout an entire document. *Alphanumeric sort* is another advanced capability; it allows you to put into alphabetical or numerical sequence such things as index entries, lists of dates, or bibliographical references. *Form letter merge* (see **merge**) can be used for research and correspondence.

export/import To *export* is to format data so that it can be used and saved in another application. To *import* is to use that data from another application. A good software application should have both capabilities.

file A collection of data in a computer that is given a name and that stores different types of information. There are several kinds of files—data files, text files, document files, program files, directory files, system files, and others.

floppy disk A thin, flexible plastic magnetic recording disk which stores computer data and documents. Often simply called *floppies,* these devices are portable. (The word *floppy* is not necessarily an accurate description, since currently used disks are more rigid than flexible.)

folder An object in a computer or on a disk that can hold multiple files and that can be used to organize documents or information.

font A complete set of type in one face, including letters, numbers, and punctuation marks.

format Format or **formatting** has to do with the way your manuscript appears on paper.

hard copy A printed copy of a manuscript or word-processing file.

hard drive A memory storage mechanism that is built into the computer; it reads and writes data onto a hard disk within the hardware itself.

input/output *Input* is data entered into a computer or word-processing system. *Output* is anything that comes out of a computer through various devices such as display screens or printers. Both words can also be used as verbs.

italics A typeface most often used for emphasis.

justify The setting of type so that the end of each line is flush right and aligned perfectly.

keyboard A computer keyboard is similar to a type-writer keyboard, but with a few extra keys.

laser printer A high-resolution printer used with computers that quickly prints either black-and-white or full-color text, photos, and graphics.

macro A series of word-processing commands and instructions that can be grouped to function as a single command to accomplish a task automatically, creating additional efficiency.

merge The creation of a form letter or document with a mailing list attached, so that when the letter and mailing list are combined, the word-processing system creates letters that appear to be personally addressed. A merge can also include envelopes and/or labels.

modem A device that is either built into the hardware or attached separately and used to interface or facilitate electronic communications.

monitor or **screen** A video display unit on which information appears when it is typed.

mouse A small manual device used to control the movement of the cursor on a computer.

PC Personal computer; a microcomputer designed with word-processing capabilities and a wide variety of additional functions, depending on what software is installed on it.

peripherals Devices, such as a modem or a printer, connected to a computer.

printer The printer produces or "outputs" the screen images onto paper. A printer is not a **stand-alone** device since it only performs from data fed into it.

program The instructions that tell a computer what to do.

software Individual computer programs or instructions that make a computer system perform spacing, remargination, repagination, automatic page numbering, and other tasks.

stand-alone system A word-processing system that is self-contained, has its own control unit and does not need any other unit to function. Most microcomputers are stand-alone devices, but printers are not because they need a computer to feed them data.

template A document with basic text, toolbars, macros, shortcut keys, styles, and other specifications already stored in it. The user can open it and create a new template or document by typing over it and saving it under a new name.

type size, point size Type size is measured in points. The higher the point number, the larger the type. Most word-processing systems have a default point size preinstalled, and unless the user changes it, every document will automatically appear in that point size.

typesetting The act of putting a manuscript into the file format to be used in its published form. The **typeset** copy is then available for proofreading on-screen or on hard copy.

typography The design and planning of printed matter through the use of type.

word-processing system Any hardware and software combination that does word-processing functions, either a specialized machine that does only word processing or a general-purpose PC that has word-processing capabilities as well as other functions. Similar to **application**.

C. Common Editing and Publishing Process Definitions

The thickness of this book would expand by several inches if we were to include an exhaustive list of terms from the publishing world. Below are definitions for terms that seem to appear most often in everyday conversations and negotiations between authors and editors:

adaptation Fiction that is converted to a screenplay.

addendum New material added to a book after its initial publication.

advance A sum paid to the author in anticipation of royalty earnings.

advance copies Prepublication edition of the book, generally used to generate reviews and publicity; also known as **ARCs (Advance Readers Copies)**.

agent Representative of an author's work to publishers, who negotiates the contract and acts as a liaison through the publishing process.

appendix Supplementary information usually printed at the back of the book.

ARC Advance Readers Copies (see **advance copies**).

authorized Written with the subject's consent.

auction An auction happens when several publishers bid for the purchase of an author's book.

back title page The side of the title page that contains copyright information and sometimes Library of Congress catalog number information and/or ISBN information.

backlist Books in print that have not been recently published.

belles lettres Literary works of aesthetic value.

bibliotherapy Denis Diderot in 1781 claimed to have

cured his wife from depression by reading (raunchy literature) to her, thus starting the new science that would later be called *bibliotherapy.*

bibliotics The study of handwriting, writing materials, and written documents to determine authenticity and authorship.

blue lines The printer's photocopy or blue print mockup of the book's pages, usually run at the end of the proof process before going to the print run. Blue lines are used to detect errors in text, photos, and graphics and make final corrections.

blue pencil A reference to an editor's corrections on a manuscript page (originally done with a blue pencil).

blurbs Cover quotes or endorsements of the book, usually by well-known writers or celebrities. Often these appear on the book jacket.

book doctor Someone hired by the author or publishing house to improve a manuscript.

clips Copies of published writing samples.

codes A system of symbols representing instructions.

colophon A publisher's logo, usually printed on the spine of a book.

copyedit To work on a manuscript prior to publication in a variety of ways and in varying degrees, including correction of spelling, grammar, usage, and other errors; organization of graphics and photographs; preparation of indexes and glossaries, and other tasks as agreed upon by the editor and author.

copy editor A person who does a variety of improvement or enhancement tasks on a book, including but not limited to enhancement of language and correction of grammar and spelling, and who also sometimes checks facts for accuracy and conformity.

copyright The author's legal right to ownership of the work under federal copyright laws; however the author doesn't always hold the copyright.

cover The outside part of the book that is not usually removable.

cover art The design of the book jacket, generally produced in-house by the publisher's art department.

cross-collateralization A contract provision that allows the publisher to charge unearned advances on a book against another title.

custom publishing The personalization of a book for an individual, group, business, or organization through an array of options including the addition of a company logo to the cover and the addition or deletion of material; advance arrangement to publish a book for a specific entity for a fee or prior purchase of a specific number of books.

desktop publishing Home office-style publishing done with ordinary word-processing equipment.

distributor A company that represents publishers by handling the warehousing and shipping of books to bookstores and libraries, usually paid by fee or commission.

earn out To sell enough copies to earn the advance against royalties.

e-book Electronic book, published in online form that can be downloaded to computers or handheld devices. See **section D, "Electronic Media Terms."**

editor Acquires the book, works with the author to develop and polish the manuscript, and champions the title through the sales and marketing process at a publishing house.

epic A larger-than-life story of a legendary hero.

epilogue A closing note following the main body of a book.

epistolary A book written in the form of letters.

faction Recently coined term used to describe works that straddle the line between fact and fiction.

fiction A story invented by the author.

final proofs Book copies that are usually stitched and wrappered; they are used often in the publisher's office and in promotion of the book.

first pages Early edition of the typeset manuscript, which is reviewed for accuracy by the author, proofreader, and project editor before publication.

first serial rights Right to excerpt a work in a periodical.

flap copy Synopses of the story, blurbs, review quotes, or other information designed to help sell the book.

flyleaf A blank page either at the front or the back of the book.

freelance Independent contractor hired to work on a book or article.

frontlist A publisher's newest book releases.

galley Bound edition of a work, often not fully corrected, available for review and publicity purposes before publication.

genre Sales and marketing category into which the title falls (e.g. mystery, suspense, Christian living, how-to, self-help).

ghostwriter Writer or cowriter who is not credited on the work.

glossary A list of definitions of words appearing throughout the book.

half title page The page that often is placed before the official title page, listing just the title of the book.

hard copy A printed copy of a manuscript or word processing file. See **section D, "Electronic Media Terms."**

imprint A distinctive line of books and possibly one of several different imprints of a publishing company.

index A directory located at the back of the book with names and terms arranged alphabetically with page numbers for easy reference.

instant book A book rushed into print that deals with a timely topic or subject.

ISBN (International Standard Book Number) The unique machine-readable identification number that the publisher assigns a specific book that distinguishes it from all other books in international publishing databases. Similar to the ISBN are **SANs** (**Standard Address Numbers** which specify an address of a member of the publishing industry) and **ISMNs** (**International Standard Music Numbers**, which identify all international printed music publications).

jacket A separately printed cover on a book, usually removable.

kill fee Amount paid to the author of an article or book which has been assigned or contracted but not slated for publication.

list position The place of publisher's importance in which a title ranks. A **lead title** will have a larger print run and bigger publicity budget than books lower on the list.

literary agent One who represents authors in the sale of publishing rights.

literati Those who have great knowledge of literature.

magnum opus An author's masterpiece or principal work.

managing or project editor Person in charge of overseeing the production of the book.

manuscript Literally, "written by hand," but unless manuscripts are referred to as **autographs**, they are not, in fact, written by hand. Rather, they are **typescripts**, the author's typing on a typewriter or word processor, and they represent the author's original draft material.

mass market Small format paperback edition.

media kit Promotional materials, such as press releases, flyers, letters, and reviews used for announcing and circulating information about a forthcoming book.

memoir Personal reflection or account.

mid-list Title or author with moderate sales appeal that does not become a best seller.

mock-up A representation of what a book will look like, especially in regard to the cover or jacket, prepared prior to the final printing and used for display purposes at a trade show or convention. A mock-up is sometimes called a **dummy**.

monograph A scholarly book on a single subject.

nonfiction Fact-based.

novella A short novel of no more than 15,000 words.

option A right the publisher retains in order to publish the author's next book.

out of print A title that is no longer maintained in the publisher's catalog or inventory.

overrun A surplus of printed books that exceeds the market demand.

P and L (profit and loss) statement The balance sheet on a title, measuring costs including author advance, production, and publicity against sales and subsidiary earnings. (Also see **proforma**.)

packager Book broker who puts together a book idea with the elements (writer, illustrator, experts, etc.) needed to bring the concept to fruition.

piracy The illegal use of copyrighted material or republishing material under copyright protection without proper permission.

point of view The perspective a story is written from.

preface Introductory text preceding the main body of a book.

prequel Recently coined term that means a book in a series set at a time prior to the existing titles.

print run Number of copies produced at one time by a publisher.

printer (as differentiated from **publisher**) In the sense of book production, the printer—or **book manufacturer**—puts the words of the book, magazine, or other product onto paper. The printer does not publish the book; publishing includes an array of a whole different set of processes. See **publisher**. The printer is not necessarily an employee of the company that publishes the book; oftentimes the printer receives a publisher's projects on a contract basis.

proforma A forecast of estimated production costs and profit for a book. Similar to **P and L** (**profit and loss**).

program The instructions that tell a computer what to do.

proofread To read and correct the typeset manuscript for minor errors, including spelling and typographical errors.

proofs Copies provided by the typesetter for the author's and publisher's inspection and correction.

proposal An author's or agent's presentation for a new book idea to a publisher.

pub date Scheduled release date for the book. Generally a title will hit the stores two weeks to a month in advance of the official release date listed in the publisher's catalog.

public domain Material no longer under copyright protection which can be reprinted without permission.

publicist Someone who customizes promotional materials for a given book or author and assists in arranging public appearances and media interviews.

publisher The publisher is responsible for all aspects of the process of releasing a book or other printed product for consumption in the designated marketplace, including acquiring, contracting, editing, printing and binding, marketing, selling, and paying of royalties. The publisher does *not* typically print the book but contracts that task to a separate entity. See **printer**.

purple prose Flowery or ornate writing using too many adjectives and adverbs.

query (1) Proposal letter from an author or agent; (2) question about textual or graphic elements of books in process sent from copy editor or proofreader to author.

remainder(s) Stock of printed but unsold books that are available for purchase in quantity at discounted prices. To *remainder* means to sell the books at deeply discounted prices.

reprint A book that is republished, usually from a hardcover to a paperback format.

returns Unsold copies returned by the bookstores or wholesalers to the publisher.

revision A rewrite of a previously published book.

royalties Percentage of the sales price earned by the author on sold copies. A royalty is a payment made to the author in exchange for granting the publisher the right to publish and sell the book.

saga A long novel following multiple generations of a group or family.

SASE Self-addressed, stamped envelope. This should be included with all submitted articles, proposals, and manuscripts.

self-published Produced by the author.

sequel A continuation of a story from an earlier book.

serial rights When a magazine or newspaper purchases the rights to publish excerpts from a book.

sidebar A column appended to an article, often boxed, that offers additional, related information and creates graphic interest.

signature In printing and binding, a *signature* is the name given to a printed sheet after it has been folded; typically a signature consists of sixteen or thirty-two pages in the book.

slush pile Unsolicited manuscripts that pile up at a publishing house.

special sales Quantity purchases of a book or publication to an individual, group, business, or organization, often at specially negotiated prices and sometimes the publication of custom editions of the book or publication.

subsidiary rights (sub rights) Sales of such rights in the book as foreign translation, first serial, audio, electronic, film, book club, and other rights as spelled out in the publishing contract. They are not as important (thus, they are subsidiary) as the primary right to publish the book.

subsidy press/publisher Publishes books for a fee, sometimes picking up part of the publication costs in order to sell and market the book through its own channels. (See **vanity press**.)

synopsis A brief description of the storyline of a novel.

title page The full page listing the title, author's name, edition, and publisher information that usually appears on the front side of the page, with the copyright information printing on the back.

tour de force A masterful work.

trade book A hardcover book of commercial appeal aimed at a general reading audience.

trade paperback The same as a trade book, except in paperback format. Also considered a less expensive alternative to hardcover publication.

trade publisher Publisher of books geared for sale to the general reading public.

trim size The physical dimensions of a book, whether 5.5" x 8.5", 6" x 9", and so on.

typesetting The act of typesetting is putting a manuscript into the designed format to be used in its published form. The *typeset* copy is then available for proofreading on-screen or on hard copy.

typography The design and planning of printed matter through the use of type.

unauthorized Without the subject's cooperation or consent.

vanity press/publisher Publishes books for a fee, usually leaving sales and marketing of the book to the author.

voice An author's distinctive writing style, including the choice of vocabulary, the tone of writing, the point of view, etc.

wholesaler A company that handles the resale of books in large quantities and serves booksellers. See **distributor**.

writer's block When an author is unable to write due to habitual procrastination, loss of confidence, lack of inspiration, and so on.

D. Electronic Media Terms

Finding acceptable or "correct" spellings for terms related to electronic media is difficult. Merriam Webster's *Collegiate Dictionary, Eleventh Edition,* does not list many of them, but many terms related to electronic media have already become parts of our everyday vocabulary. Following are some short definitions and suggested spellings for common terms related to electronic publishing, words that you may want to use in either text or citations, and words that are being appropriated with special or new meanings for electronic usage.

blog Jargon term, short for "Web log"; a Web page that serves as a publicly accessible, often personalized individual journal.

bulletin board An electronic information and data transfer service that can be accessed by a computer terminal through its modem and the telecommunications software.

byte Basic unit of computer information storage. (See **gigabyte**, **kilobyte**, and **megabyte**.)

CD-ROM Abbreviation for *Compact Disk Read-Only Memory*; laser disk that stores digital information for computer retrieval.

chat acronyms Abbreviations of words used primarily in chat rooms while instant messaging. They have become a popular shorthand for common phrases that people say. Seen in e-mail, text messages, news-group postings, discussion boards, and now in all types of media. Examples might be BFN (Bye for now), BRB (Be right back), SUL8R (See you later), TTFN (Ta ta for now).

chat room A virtual room where a chat session takes place. Technically, a chat room is really a channel, but the term *room* is used to promote the chat metaphor.

cyberspace A metaphor for describing the nonphysical terrain created by computer systems. Online systems create a cyberspace within which people can communicate by e-mail, do research, shop, or even take classes.

cyberspeak The specialized or reappropriated language of the Internet.

domain A group of computers and devices on a network that are administered as a unit with common rules and procedures.

dot-com Slang term for Internet-based companies, i.e., "The company, which was a dot-com, went out of business." Comes from the last part of a commercial URL, which is ".com."

download Noun: The transfer of data from a computer or telecommunications network to another computer or other electronic device or storage medium. Verb: To transfer the data or information.

e-*anything* An "e" placed before a word or phrase stands for "electronic." For example, an *e-book* is an electronic version of a book. Hyphenating the word after the *e* sometimes helps its readability. It is helpful, for example, to hyphenate *e-commerce, e-publishing,* and so on. There are other terms such as "etailing" and "ecruiting" that are plays on traditional words and should not be hyphenated. See **e-mail**.

e-book or ebook A book that can be downloaded and read on a computer or other digital device.

e-mail or email Noun: Electronic mail. Verb: to send electronic mail. Do not capitalize.

e-publishing To display, present, or post some type of written, auditory, or visual media on the World Wide Web. Many newspapers and magazines now e-publish an electronic version of their publication on the Web.

e-zine or zine An electronic version of a publisher's magazine. Similar to an **e-journal**.

firewall A system in computer hardware, software, or both that is designed to prevent unauthorized access to or from a private network. It examines messages and blocks ones that do not meet specified security criteria.

FTP Abbreviation of File Transfer Protocol, the protocol used on the Internet for sending files.

geek A popular term used to describe a person who knows a lot about computers and/or the Internet. It used to be considered somewhat derogatory to call someone a *geek*, but now that the Internet has made computer usage mainstream, the connotation is not as negative.

Do not put this term or other similar ones in quotation marks.

gigabyte (Gb or GB) Unit of computer measurement equal to one billion bytes or a thousand megabytes.

gonk Verb: To embellish the truth beyond reasonable recognition, imported from the German word *gonken. Du gonkst mir* means "You're pulling my leg." In cyberspeak, the usage is "You're gonking me."

Google Verb, capitalized: To look up online information about a person, place, or thing, from the popular Google Web search engine.

hacker A computer enthusiast who explores computer systems and programs to the point of obsession, often used to describe persons who use their knowledge to cause harm or damage to computer systems. Do not put in quotation marks.

hard copy Printed copy of some kind of information (as opposed to an electronic version). You'll hear someone ask, "Do you have a hard copy of that?" The electronic version is known as a "soft copy."

host A computer system that is accessed by a user working at a remote location, or a computer that is connected to a TCP/IP network, including the Internet.

HTML Abbreviation for *HyperTest Markup Language,* the language used to create documents on the World Wide Web.

HTTP Abbreviation for *HyperText Transfer Protocol,* the underlying protocol used by the World Wide Web, abbreviated as HTTP. It defines how messages are formatted and transmitted and what actions Web servers and browsers should take in response to various commands.

instant message or **IM** Noun or verb. Noun: Instantaneous communication that enables a person to create a private chat room with another person. Verb, in everyday usage: "I'm going to instant message (IM) Susie as soon as she gets online."

Internet, (the) Network infrastructure that connects computers around the world. Be sure to capitalize this word.

in the zone A state in which one shuts out all forms of communication because the person is entirely focused on, and extremely busy with, his work.

intranet A private network, within a company or organization, that serves shared applications intended for internal use only. Do not capitalize.

IP Abbreviation of *Internet protocol,* pronounced as two separate letters. IP by itself is something like the postal system. It allows you to address a package and drop it in the system, but there's no direct link between you and the recipient. TCP/IP, on the other hand, establishes a connection between two hosts so that they can send messages back and forth for a period of time.

IT Short for *information technology,* and pronounced as separate letters; the broad subject concerned with all aspects of managing and processing information, especially within a large organization or company.

kilobyte A unit of measurement that equals a little over one thousand bytes.

mailbox The directory where your host computer stores your e-mail messages.

megabyte (Mb or MB) Unit of computer measurement equal to more than a thousand kilobytes and more than a million bytes.

morph or **morphing** In cyberspeak, to transform one image into another by a gradual distortion of the first image. Special effects *morphing* is the video technique in which one image slowly changes into another on the screen. In popular current usage, to turn from one thing into another. Though *morph* and *morphing* have their roots in the verb *metamorphose* and its noun form *metamorphosis,* the words have taken on lives of their own outside of the cyberspeak arena and their current usages do not reflect the definitions in a standard dictionary.

nanosecond A unit of time representing one-billionth of a second.

nerd Similar to a geek; a brainy person who knows nearly everything there is to know about computers. People used to make fun of those who were considered to be nerds, but now some people think that calling someone a nerd is a compliment.

Netiquette The code of conduct and unofficial rules that govern online interaction and behavior. This word is usually capitalized.

newsgroup Public bulletin board on the Internet; collectively known as "Usenet."

online (not *on-line*) Via, within, or on the Internet: "I'm going to chat with him online." "*The Tennessean* publishes an online newspaper."

paradigm shift The acceptance by a majority of people of a changed belief or attitude or way of doing something. For example, "Getting people to read LifeWay's *Adult EXTRA!* online instead receiving a hard copy in the mail is going to require a major paradigm shift." NOTE: This term is close to cliché status, so be careful when using it.

quantum leap A big move forward, a positive stride, an improvement. NOTE: This phrase is getting close to cliché status, so be careful when using it.

RAM Abbreviation for *Random Access Memory*; the short-term memory a computer needs to store the information it is processing at any given moment.

ramp up The modern equivalent of getting psyched. Ramping up can also refer to the time you need to learn enough about a job or project to work effectively on it. For example, "The ramp up time on the new organizational structure is one month. The implementation committee will present its six-step plan in one week."

scan Verb: To digitize an image by passing it through an optical scanner. Noun: the image itself, i.e., "She scanned the architect's design in the scanner and then sent a copy of the scan to the church council."

smiley A sequence of typed characters that creates a rough picture of something, such as a facial expression. Examples: :-) for a smile, :- (for a frown.

snail mail Regular postal mail. Also called (not as commonly) "p-mail."

spam An e-mail message sent to a large number of people without consent, also known as Unsolicited Commercial E-mail (UCE) or junk e-mail. Spam is usually sent to promote a product or service. Common spams are chain letters, pyramid schemes, stock offerings from unknown corporations, quack health products, and pornographic solicitations.

TCP Abbreviation of *Transmission Control Protocol*; one of the main protocols in TCP/IP networks. (See **IP**.)

upload To transmit data from a computer to a bulletin board service, mainframe or network.

URL Abbreviation for *Uniform Resource Locator;* World Wide Web address of an Internet resource. Example: http://www.lifeway.com. There is no good reason to italicize or underline URLs in text or in notes.

virus A small program, commonly embedded in another program or in a communication that infects other programs, communications, data, drives, or disks, causing them to malfunction.

Web site (not *website*) A location on the World Wide Web that contains a home page and possibly additional files. In this case as in most others, capitalize *Web*.

World Wide Web or **the Web** or **WWW** The way of accessing information over the Internet through selecting hypertext links between text or graphics and other Web pages or Internet resources. Not a synonymous term with "the Internet."

Words derived from World Wide Web The spelling of words and phrases derived from the term *World Wide Web* has no obvious logic. Following is a list of derivatives and their most commonly used spellings:

Web bug	Web space
Web content	Web tone
Web designer	Webcam
Web developer	webcasting
Web graffiti	webcentric
Web guide	WebCrawler
Web guru	webify
Web hippie	Webisode
Web hosting	Webmail
Web jam	Webmaster
Web marketplace	Webmistress

Web page	WebRing
Web presentations	Websmith
Web ratings	webster
Web server	webtop
Web site	

CHAPTER 10
Proofreading and Editing Marks and Explanations (3.20–.36)

PUNCTUATION MARKS		TYPOGRAPHICAL SIGNS	
⌄	Insert comma	*ital*	Set in italic type
⌄ ⌄	Insert apostrophe *or* single quotation mark	*rom*	Set in roman type
⟨⟨ ⟩⟩	Insert quotation marks	*bf*	Set in boldface type
⊙	Insert period	*lc*	Set in lowercase
(set) ?	Insert question mark	*caps*	Set in capital letters
;	Insert semicolon	*sc*	Set in small capitals
⌃ or :│	Insert colon	*wf*	Wrong font; set in correct type
⹀	Insert hyphen	X	Check type image; remove blemish
M	Insert em dash	V	Insert here *or* make superscript
N	Insert en dash	Λ	Insert here *or* make subscript
€│∄or (│)	Insert parentheses		

OPERATIONAL SIGNS

ℐ	Delete
◠	Close up; delete space
ℐ⌣	Delete and close up (use only when deleting letters *within* a word)
stet	Let it stand
#	Insert space
eq #	Make space between words equal; make space between lines equal
hr #	Insert hair space
ls	Letterspace
¶	Begin new paragraph
☐	Indent type one em from left or right
⌐	Move right
⌐	Move left
⌐⌐	Center
⊓	Move up
⊔	Move down
fl	Flush left
fr	Flush right
=	Straighten type; align horizontally
‖	Align vertically
tr	Transpose
ⓢⓟ	Spell out

CHAPTER 11
Writing for
Christian Publishers

Evangelical Christian publishers are committed to publishing books that help bring people to a personal knowledge of God through Jesus Christ, that help them grow stronger in their Christian walk, that help them understand and live in a world becoming increasingly hostile to Christianity, that bring biblical reality to them in stories relating Christian experiences to contemporary life and ideas, that examine crucial issues through a Christian worldview, and that show God's sovereignty and work consistently to glorify God.

Each book published for the Christian reading audience needs to be consistent with what the Bible teaches and not stand in conflict with Scripture in any way. Each book should stand within the stream of historic Christian truth as affirmed by genuine Christians through the ages and reaffirmed in classic evangelical orthodoxy and its heritage. Each book needs to be in accord with the publishing company's statement of faith. And Christian publishers need to have a clear sense that the author of each book they publish is a sincere Christian seeking to live a consistent Christian life.

Most editorial departments make an initial assessment of book manuscripts (and sometimes even the final publishing decision) on the basis of formal book proposals and not on unsolicited manuscripts. Therefore, do not send unsolicited manuscripts to them. Instead, send a four-to-six page typed proposal that includes the following:

1. The purpose of your proposed book
2. The nature and scope of each chapter
3. The anticipated manuscript length and the scheduled completion date of the first draft of the writing project
4. What research is required and how you intend to research your subject
5. Information on the target or intended reading audience
6. A comparison of your book to other published books on the same subject or similar subjects
7. A brief autobiographical summary telling why you are qualified to write the book.

Include with the proposal two sample chapters, clearly legible, double-spaced, and with consecutively numbered pages on 8.5" x 11" sheets. Be sure to include a self-addressed, stamped envelope. If publishers are potentially interested in publishing your book, they will request additional material. If they do request more material, always include a self-addressed, stamped mailer for the return of the manuscript should they decide that it is not what is needed.

How do you know if you might be interested in writing for a particular publishing house? First, determine what category you think your book will fall into. Is it biography or business? Is it church life or Christian living? Are you writing a novel? Are you writing a book for Christian education or counseling? Is your book about evangelism? Are you writing on the cults, how to have family devotions, church history, or humor? Is your book a text that could be used in a college course on apologetics or a seminary course on hermeneutics? And so on. You have to figure out in your own mind just what you are doing. Then you need to find reference material in a good library that will help you locate publishers that publish the kind of book you are writing. This essentially is market research, and you need to do it so that you are sending your proposal only to publishers whose list matches the book you are interested in writing. What kind of reference material can you find? Look for periodically updated guides to the religious book markets. For example, in most good libraries you can find volumes such as *The Writer's Market* and the *Literary Market Place*. These volumes and others like them will show you what kinds of books a given publisher specializes in. They also list requirements for submission and will most likely include an address and phone number of the house, along with the names of the acquisition editors in many cases. You should study these books closely and determine which publishers you think would be interested in your writing project. You need to show the editors that you have done a thorough a job of research *before* you contact them.

You can also find in many Christian bookstores some volumes that will give you the same kind of information on specifically *Christian* publishers. You might check, for example, *The Christian Writer's Market Guide* or

The Christian Writer's Book: A Practical Guide to Writing. With these kinds of tools in hand, you will know what the publishing vision and editorial model is of the house you have in mind and whether it seems appropriate for your particular project.

Next, write publishers and request their guidelines, enclosing a self-addressed, stamped envelope. After studying each one's editorial model and guidelines for submission, if you still believe that one or more seems to be an appropriate publisher for your work, send a query letter to each that describes who you are, what your book is about, what makes your book unique from any others like it already published, and why you think it fits that company's publishing program. A letter such as this should be one to two typed (double-spaced) pages. Along with the query letter, send the proposal outlined above. Be sure to follow closely the requirements for submission. It is to your advantage if your proposal and manuscript are tailored to each publishing company's specific guidelines.

Careful preparation of the letter, proposal, and manuscript samples is vital. Be sure everything is in presentable form, typewritten, and free of spelling and grammatical errors before you send it. Editors do not wish to receive materials that are hastily thrown together, or in such rough-draft form that they cannot discern their true quality. When asked to submit material in electronic form, remember that completed manuscripts need to be submitted on a 3.5-inch disk compatible to either IBM or Macintosh computers. Much word processing is done in Microsoft Word, although most publishers do have the ability to convert from other programs. It is important to indicate which program you have used for your manuscript.

Some general questions editors ask when considering a manuscript include the following: What makes this book unique, significant, and important? What specific contribution does this book make? In what way does this book have something distinctively Christian to say? Is there a real need for this book? Will it help people to have a deeper understanding of their faith? Will it help readers live more effectively as Christians? What kind of distribution do we think this book will have? Will sales be large enough to make the book commercially viable? If the distribution potential is not large enough, should we publish it anyway because of the importance of its message? What kind of financial and other commitments are involved in securing the project, in production, and in promotion? Do we have the personnel and financial resources to publish this effectively? What is the potential for this author, in relation to both this project and other projects? Can we perform a real service for this author in realizing the potential of this project and in helping the author develop his or her gifts for the publication of future books? Do we have the necessary commitment within our staff to do our best in the publication of this book? All things considered, do we believe that this is something the Lord would have us publish?

CHAPTER 12
Suggested Books for Authors and Editors

A. Grammar, Style, and Usage

Amis, Kingsley. *The King's English: A Guide to Modern Usage.* New York: St. Martins Press, 1998. "Not every Americanism deserves to have its credentials carefully examined. Some ought to be shot on sight." A British teasing of aspects of Americanisms and the smearing of meanings.

Baker, Sheridan. *The Complete Stylist,* 3rd ed. New York: Harper and Row, Publishers, 1989. A justly famous textbook on expository writing that has been used by many thousands of students since it originally appeared in 1966. From the larger concept of rhetoric to the more focused rhetorical problems of paragraphs, sentences, punctuation, and words. The text does many additional things, such as surveying the advantages and pitfalls of logic and tour the library.

Bernstein, Theodore M. *The Careful Writer: A Modern Guide to English Usage,* 3rd ed. New York: Atheneum,

1995. A concise handbook that handles over two thousand alphabetical listings of words and concepts that usually give writers pause, covering questions of use, grammar, punctuation, precision, logical structure, and color.

Bernstein, Theodore M. *Dos, Don'ts & Maybes of English Usage*. New York: Random House, 1999. Highly competent usage advice.

Bernstein, Theodore M. *Miss Thistlebottom's Hobgoblins: The Careful Writer's Guide to the Taboos, Bugbears and Outmoded Rules of English Usage*. New York: Farrar, Straus & Giroux Inc., 1991. By the author of *The Careful Writer.* Bernstein shows how Miss Thistlebottom and others who teach the "rules" of grammar are sometimes wrong about what makes good English and especially wrong about accepting certain taboos that lack any historical, logical, or grammatical basis.

The Chicago Manual of Style, 15th ed. Prepared by the editorial staff of the University of Chicago Press. Chicago: University of Chicago Press, 2003. This justly famous volume is the standard reference tool, essential guide, and primary authority for all authors, editors, copywriters, and proofreaders. Covers editing, grammar, style, usage, production, and printing. *The Chicago Manual* settles most disputes over usage and grammar and is called "the bible of the book business."

Claiborne, Robert. *Saying What You Mean: A Commonsense Guide to American Usage*. New York: Ballantine Books, 1987. A usage expert who gets behind why a given word or construction is good or bad.

Donahue, Mary Lee. *The Harbrace College Handbook,* 12th ed. San Diego, Calif.: Harcourt Brace Jovanovich,

1994. A classic and easy-to-follow classroom text on grammar, punctuation, spelling, diction, and more.

Douglas, Auriel and Michael Strumpf. *Webster's New World Guide to Punctuation.* New York: Prentice Hall/Simon & Schuster, 1988. All the rules you need to know to punctuate correctly.

Dumond, Val. *The Elements of Nonsexist Usage: A Guide to Inclusive Spoken and Written English.* New York: Prentice Hall Press/Simon & Schuster, Inc., 1991. A brief handbook for anyone wanting to eliminate sexism from their spoken and written English. Good material on the way to circumvent sexist writing and good glossary of alternative terms.

Eller, Vernard. *The Language of Canaan and the Grammar of Feminism.* Grand Rapids, Mich.: Wm. B. Eerdmans Publishing Company, 1982. A brave and intelligent *defense* of "sexist" language as it relates to trying to move our God-language beyond gender. Explores whether many feminists are competent in "the language of Canaan," and studies the theological, philosophical, and anthropological bases underlying hard-shell feminism.

Ferguson, Don K. *Grammar Gremlins.* Lakewood, Colo.: Glenbridge Publishing, Ltd., 1995. Handles nagging grammar and usage questions to help writers and editors in punctuation, spelling, grammar, usage, pronunciation, etc. The information in this book was collected through various teachers' groups the author has addressed in many venues.

Follett, Wilson. *Modern American Usage: A Guide,* rev. ed. New York: Crown Publishers, 1981. All writers and editors should have this famous and wide-ranging volume on their shelf for reference.

Fowler, H. W.; rev. by Sir Ernest Gowers. *A Dictionary of Modern English Usage,* 2nd ed. Oxford: Oxford University Press, 1965. Dated now but still full of wonderful essays on grammar, style, and language use.

Gallagher, Nora. *How to Stop a Sentence (and Other Methods of Managing Words).* New York: HarperCollins Publishers, 1985. A fun and foundational guide to good punctuation, useful for the novice as brush-up. The theme is on using punctuation as a matter of common sense—using the mark that feels right.

Gibaldi, Joseph. *MLA Handbook for Writers of Research Papers,* 6th ed. New York: Modern Language Association, 2003. A new edition of the handbook that has been used by millions of writers. This authoritative manual to MLA style presents a comprehensive guide to preparing research papers, including information on using computers for research and writing and on citing electronic publications.

Goldstein, Norm, et al, ed. *The Associated Press Stylebook and Libel Manual,* updated and revised. Reading, Mass.: Addison-Wesley Publishing Company, 1998. Authoritative word on the rules of grammar, punctuation, and the general meaning and usage of thousands of terms.

Good, C. Edward. *A Grammar Book for You and I (. . . Oops, Me!).* Sterling, Va.: Capital Books, 2002. This valuable book covers the parts of speech, punctuation, and common grammatical mistakes, and guides the user toward communicating with clarity and style.

Gordon, Karen Elizabeth. *The Deluxe Transitive Vampire: The Ultimate Handbook of Grammar for the*

Innocent, the Eager, and the Doomed, Updated Edition. New York: Pantheon Books, 1993. Intelligent and whimsical guide out of the linguistic labyrinth. William Safire called this "a book to sink your fangs into."

Hairston, Maxine, John J. Ruszkiewicz, and Christy Friend. *The Scott, Foresman Handbook for Writers,* 6th ed. New York: Longman, 2001. Lively expert help for writers in mastering the conventions of standard English, including an overview of the writing process and sections on style, mechanics, usage, research and writing tools. The handbook has helpful marginal symbols that mark items of composition and usage on a research-based scale of priorities.

Hudson, Bob and Shelley Townsend. *A Christian Writer's Manual of Style.* Grand Rapids, Mich.: Zondervan Publishing House, 1988. This complete manual will be published in a revised and enlarged form in 2004. It is unique because the examples are taken from Scripture, church history, and Christian literature. This manual encourages those who work professionally with words to awake to the significant spiritual implications of our language.

Johnson, Edward D. *The Handbook of Good English,* rev. ed. New York: Facts on File, 1991. Excellent sections on composition, diction, grammar, punctuation, and style.

Kipfer, Barbara Ann, ed. *21st Century Manual of Style.* New York: Dell Publishing, 1995. An alternative style guide that is arranged in a convenient A-to-Z dictionary format and combines the rules found in standard style-books. Rolls the essentials of the dictionary, thesaurus, and grammar book into one reference volume.

Maggio, Rosalie. *Dictionary of Bias-Free Usage: A Guide to Nondiscriminatory Language*. Phoenix, Ariz: The Oryx Press, 1992. Tips on how to avoid sexist, racist, and ageist language, organized in alphabetical order.

Miller, Casey and Kate Swift. *The Handbook of Nonsexist Writing for Writers, Editors and Speakers,* 2nd ed. New York: Harper Collins Publishers, 1988. Useful and sensible suggestions on avoiding unconscious sexual bias and outright sexist connotations in writing.

Miller, Casey and Kate Swift. *Words and Women: New Language in New Times,* updated ed. Garden City, N.Y.: HarperCollins Publishers, 1991. A summary of the question of sex stereotyping in language, with evidence drawn from the language itself.

Mitchell, Richard. *Less Than Words Can Say.* Boston: Trafalgar Square, 2000. A funny and irreverent indictment of the misuse of the English language from the publisher of the equally irreverent newsletter, *The Underground Grammarian.*

Morris, William and Mary Morris. *The Harper Dictionary of Contemporary Usage,* 2nd ed. New York: HarperCollins Publishers, 1992. The authors were assisted by a panel of 136 distinguished consultants on usage. Informative, fascinating, and expert guidance on the latest trends in our constantly changing language. Good discussion of sexism in language and of effective ways to deal with it. Hundreds of questions on usage, with sharp debates among the consultants.

Newman, Edwin. *A Civil Tongue.* New York: Warner Books, 1983. A follow-up to his best-selling *Strictly Speaking,* this is a logical, funny, and clever attack on the way writers, journalists, academics, bureaucrats, politicians, and others misuse English.

O'Conner, Patricia T. *Woe Is I: The Grammarphobe's Guide to Better English in Plain English.* New York: Putnam Publishing Group, 1996. Popular and painless instruction on grammar and plain English usage.

O'Conner, Patricia T. *Words Fail Me.* New York: Harcourt, 1999. Lighthearted grammar guide and writing primer.

Opdycke, John B. *Harper's English Grammar,* rev. ed. New York: Warner Books, 1991. A clear and complete introduction to all phases of good grammar, with a blending of traditional rules and later developments. An excellent index allows the reader to go directly to specific entries.

Partridge, Eric. *The Wordsworth Book of Usage & Abusage.* Ware, Hertfordshire, Eng.: Wordsworth Editions, 1995. Condensed from the author's *Usage and Abusage: A Guide to Good English* and first published in 1954 as *The Concise Usage and Abusage,* this is—as the cover tagline says—the famous guide to good English. A fascinating work by a famous philologist and lexicographer.

Partridge, Eric; James Whitcut, ed. *Usage and Abusage: A Guide to Good English.* New York: W.W. Norton and Company, 1995. Packed with historical, cultural. and literary information, along with the basics of grammar, this book steers the reader away from confusions between words and toward clarity and directness of expression.

Pinckert, Robert C. *Pinckert's Practical Grammar: A Lively, Unintimidating Guide to Usage, Punctuation and Style.* Cincinnati, Ohio: Writer's Digest Books, 1991. Sometimes the study of grammar, usage, and punctuation appears rule-ridden and stiff. This book offers helpful examples, lists, quizzes, and other devices that help clarify usage and reinforce strong sentences and paragraphs.

Randall, Bernice. *Webster's New World Guide to Current American Usage.* New York: Webster's New World/Simon & Schuster, 1988. A genuinely helpful book on usage, from grammar and punctuation to the different directions American English is taking in the twenty-first century. Covers the idioms and the slang that have come into the language and the linguistic principles of assimilation. Includes an extensive analysis of current trends.

Ross-Larson, Bruce. *Edit Yourself.* New York: W. W. Norton & Company, 1985. Help in making one's writing clear and concise; includes a list of common errors to avoid.

Safire, William. *On Language.* New York: Times Books, 1987. Safire, political columnist for *The New York Times,* enlightens readers on proper English grammar and usage, correct pronunciation, slang, neologisms, jargon, the roots of our words, and much more. All taken from his famous column "On Language."

Safire, William. *Take My Word for It.* New York: Times Books, 1988. The author of *On Language* offers this second volume of advice on words and usage taken from his nationally syndicated "On Language" column in *The New York Times.*

Shertzer, Margaret. *The Elements of Grammar.* New York: Longman, 1996. An authoritative and thorough guide to good grammar and a companion to Strunk and White's *The Elements of Style.* Hundreds of examples of correct grammar drawn from contemporary writers.

Siegel, Allan M. and William G. Connolly. *The New York Times Manual of Style and Usage,* rev. and expanded. New York: Three Rivers Press, 1999. This is the stylebook used by the editors and writers of *The New York Times,* but it is a desk book for all editors and writers. A sure guide (especially for article writing and other nonbook writing) for accuracy and consistency on matters of spelling, punctuation, English usage, overall writing quality, and much more.

Skillin, Marjorie E., et al. *Words into Type,* 3rd ed. Englewood Cliffs, N.J.: Prentice-Hall, 1986. All those connected to writing, editing, publishing, typesetting—in short, those connected with putting words into type—should have this volume, but especially copy editors will benefit from it. It is a treasure trove of information on countless areas such as grammar rules, punctuation, style guidelines, preparing manuscripts, copy editing, typography, and printing, One reviewer called this about half a dozen textbooks rolled into one.

Smith, Ken. *Grammar, Style, and Usage.* New York: Blast Books, 2001. Shows how mindless jargon, euphemisms, and weasel words poison the reservoir of good English.

Stilman, Anne. *Grammatically Correct: The Writer's Essential Guide to Punctuation, Spelling, Style, Usage, and Grammar.* Cincinnati, Ohio: Writer's Digest Books, 1977. Practical instruction on how to write accurately, clearly, and gracefully.

Strunk, Jr., William I. and E. B. White. *The Elements of Style,* 4th ed. New York: Allyn & Bacon, 2000. The most acclaimed and indispensable small style manual. Always have it on hand.

Tracz, Richard Francis. *Dr. Grammar's Writes from Wrongs.* New York: Vintage Books/Random House, Inc., 1991. As "Dr. Grammar," the author directs The Write Line, an English-language telephone hotline. This book is an excellent guide to the common and not-so-common rules of our language.

U.S. Government Printing Office Style Manual, rev. ed. Washington, D.C.: U.S. Government Printing Office, 2000. For writers and editors who work for government publications, this is the standard guide. But all editors and writers will find it useful, especially for the list of official government abbreviations.

van Leunen, Mary-Claire. *A Handbook for Scholars,* 2nd ed. New York: Oxford University Press, 1992. An alternative to the traditional stylebooks. Good advice on footnoting, bibliography, and manuscript preparation. Excellent reference as a style guide for editors who prepare scholarly texts.

Walsh, Bill. *Lapsing into a Comma.* New York: The McGraw-Hill Companies, 2000. Humorous, entertaining commentary and stylebook that addresses usage topics, obscure words, and slang expressions, written by the copy chief for the *Washington Post's* business desk.

Williams, Joseph M. *Style: Ten Lessons in Clarity and Grace,* 7th ed. New York: Longman, 2002. Extremely valuable prescriptive help in eliminating the tangled, overly complex type of prose and in communicating writing that is comprehensible, clear, and precise. The author, a professor of English at the University of Chicago, does not cover all the problems of form and composition but focuses rather on style.

B. Dictionaries, Thesauruses, and Other Reference Books

The American Heritage Dictionary of the English Language, 4th ed. Boston: Houghton Mifflin, 2000. Highly regarded for its word histories and regional notes. Considered more permissive than other dictionaries. Almost 200,000 main entries and over 500 separate notes on usage.

Aycock, Don M. and Leonard George Goss. *The Christian Writer's Book: A Practical Guide to Writing.* North Brunswick, N.J.: Bridge-Logos Publishers, 1996. A practical, easy-to read, common-sense manual, resource guide, and reference book, designed to help Christian writers and editors understand the nonfiction publishing process.

Aycock, Don M. and Leonard George Goss. *Writing Religiously: A Guide to Writing Nonfiction Religious Books.* Grand Rapids, Mich.: Baker Book House, 1984. Here is a full set of tools helping writers at all stages translate the creative imagination into written words. Shares the excitement of the religious book field on an intimate, personal basis with the reader and offers much good advice about writing and being published.

Ayto, John. *Dictionary of Word Origins.* New York: Arcade Publishing, 1993. Intriguing and authoritative history of words and their derivations for all word lovers and those fascinated by language.

Bartlett, John. *Bartlett's Familiar Quotations,* 17th ed. Boston: Little, Brown, 2002. For checking the accuracy of quotations, this is the editor's first recourse. A usable index allows one to find a quotation with just a key word or phrase.

Barzun, Jacques and Henry F. Graff. *The Modern Researcher,* 5th ed. San Diego, Calif.: Harcourt Brace Jonanovich, 1992. This book is a standard in the field of research. The authors offer a thorough guide to fact-gathering and interpretation. Read this one.

Beard, Henry and Christopher Cerf. *The Official Politically Correct Dictionary and Handbook.* New York: Villard Books, 1993. For both oppressors and victims, this book on the new appropriateness tells you exactly what's OK to say to whom, what you can't say, who says so, and why. It is hilarious, except that when one discovers all the entries come from actual use in magazines, books, speeches, etc., it becomes quite chilling. This book shows that "language is not merely the mirror of our society; it is the major force in 'constructing' what we perceive as 'reality.'" Changing our language means changing everything.

Bowler, Peter. *The Superior Person's Book of Words.* Boston: David R. Godine, Publisher, 1998. This book provides the men or women in the street with better verbal weapons so they can become superior people—whose vocabulary is "a badge of rank as compelling as a top hat or a painted forehead." Five hundred outrageous entries.

Bowler, Peter. *The Superior Person's Second Book of Weird and Wondrous Words.* Boston: David R. Godine, Publisher, 1992. Six hundred new words as outlandish as the ones in the previous volume.

Brandreth, Gyles. *The Joy of Lex: How to Have Fun with 860,341,500 Words.* New York: Quill/William Morrow and Company, 2002. For word freaks and lexicon lovers. Shows our language can be endlessly fascinating and fun.

Brownstone, David M. and Irene M. Franck. *The Dictionary of Publishing.* New York: Van Nostrand Reinhold Company, 1982. The peculiar language of publishing includes definitions from many fields, including printing, journalism, art, photography, computer science, sales, marketing, bookselling, the old and rare books field, business and finance, law, accounting, administration, distribution, insurance and library studies. Here is an excellent reference aid to help one keep up.

Bryson, Bill. *Bryson's Dictionary of Troublesome Words.* New York: Broadway Books, 2002. Concise A-to-Z guide to usage, spelling, grammar, and punctuation.

Bryson, Bill. *The Mother Tongue: English and How It Got That Way.* New York: Avon Books, 1996. Entertaining and anecdotal survey of the crazy language we call English.

Bryson, Bill. *The Penguin Dictionary for Writers and Editors,* reprint ed. New York: Penguin Books/Viking, 1995. This quick guide through spelling and usage controversies of the English language is useful for writers, journalists, secretaries, copy editors, editors, and publishers.

Bryson, Bill. *The Penguin Dictionary of Troublesome Words,* 2nd ed. New York: Viking Press, 1988. Guidance handbook on the pitfalls and disputed issues in standard written English. Also includes a glossary of grammatical terms and an appendix on punctuation.

Buchanan-Brown, John, et al. *Le Mot Juste: A Dictionary of Classical and Foreign Words and Phrases,* reprint ed. New York: Vintage Books, 1991. This small lexicon carries hundreds of words and phrases from Greek, Latin, French, German, Italian, Spanish, Russian, and Yiddish that have been introduced into our language but that nevertheless are often confused and misused. For the writer tired of making faux pas and looking like a dummkopf. Phonetic spellings for proper pronunciation are included.

Burchfield, Robert W., ed. *The Compact Edition of the Oxford English Dictionary.* New York: Oxford University Press, 1987. A two-volume microprint edition of the twelve-volume *Oxford English Dictionary,* the only dictionary that traces the development of a word from its first appearance. A diffuse dictionary for scholarly use and probably not for the daily use of writers and editors who need to find current meanings quickly.

Carter, John; rev. by Nicolas Barker. *A B C for Book Collectors,* 7th ed. New Castle, Del.: Oak Knoll Press, 2000. This is an entertaining and basic reference tool containing definitions and analyses of more than 450 technical terms having to do with bookmaking, book collecting, and bibliography.

Chantrell, Glynnis, ed. *The Oxford Dictionary of Word Histories.* New York: Oxford University Press, 2002. Describes the origins and sense development of over 11,000 core words of the English language. For language aficionados and linguistic history buffs.

Ciardi, John. *A Second Browser's Dictionary and Native's Guide to the Unknown American Language.* New York: HarperCollins Publishers, 1983. Ciardi goes beyond the standard dictionaries and offers an enlightening and entertaining book for browsing, full of intimate conversation with words and phrases and their origins and shifting histories.

Ciardi, John. *A Third Browser's Dictionary: A Compendium of Curious Expressions & Intriguing Facts.* North

Pomfret, Vt.: Trafalgar Square Books, 2001. Another Ciardi resource for ardent logophiles.

Curl, Michael. *The Wordsworth Dictionary of Anagrams.* Ware, Hertfordshire, Eng.: Wordsworth Editions, 1995. This was originally published in 1982 as *The Anagram Dictionary.* Anagrams have come to be associated with mystical properties. This reference source includes a history of anagrams from the Greeks and Romans and lists twenty thousand words which are arranged alphabetically, with all their known anagrams. For lovers of all word games.

Devlin, Joseph; edited and enlarged by Jerome Fried. *A Dictionary of Synonyms and Antonyms,* reissue ed. New York: Popular Library, Inc./Warner Books, Inc., 1987. Help in finding just the right word for fresh written and spoken expression. Includes five thousand words most often mispronounced.

Ehrlich, Eugene. *The Harper Dictionary of Foreign Terms,* 3rd ed. New York: HarperCollins Publishers, 1987. This edition is based on the 1934 classic edition compiled by C. O. Sylvester Mawson. Here one finds definitions of more than fifteen thousand foreign words and expressions from more than fifty different languages that Americans frequently use in their conversation and writing.

Ehrlich Eugene. *The Highly Selective Dictionary of Golden Adjectives for the Extraordinarily Literate.* New York: HarperResource, 2002. More than 850 adjectives finally get the treatment they deserve. For writers, editors, speakers, and word buffs.

Ehrlich, Eugene, et al., comp. *Oxford American Dictionary,* reissue ed. New York: Avon, 1983. Compact guide to American English. Includes slang, informal words, and technical words and phrases. The OAD is based on the *Oxford Paperback Dictionary*.

Farb, Peter. *Word Play: What Happens When People Talk,* reprint ed. New York: Alfred A. Knopf, 1993. The author proposes that language represents twin systems of grammar and human behavior.

Feather, John. *A Dictionary of Book History*. New York: Oxford University Press, 1996. This is a handbook of articles for scholars, editors, bibliophiles, research students, librarians, and booksellers on the history of books, book collectors and collecting, printing and bookselling. Includes notes for further research.

Fiske, Robert Hartwell. *Thesaurus of Alternatives to Worn-out Words and Phrases*. Cincinnati, Ohio: Writer's Digest Books, 1994. Help in getting rid of moribund metaphors, torpid terms, and wretched redundancies. This book offers many good replacements for shopworn expressions, with advice on how to keep your writing fresh.

Fowler, H. W., ed. *The Concise Oxford Dictionary of Current English*, 9th ed. Oxford: Oxford University Press, 1995. With British spellings and the British meanings for words, this is an accessible, authoritative, and concise reference tool.

Funk, Charles Earle. *A Hog on Ice and Other Curious Expressions*. New York: HarperResource, 2002. Funk takes over four hundred expressions and sayings that we use in everyday speech and traces the meanings back through the years. By the author of *Thereby Hangs a Tale*.

Funk, Charles Earle. *Thereby Hangs a Tale: Stories of Curious Word Origins*. New York: HarperResource, 2002.

Examines hundreds of words in common English that acquired their meanings in strange and unusual ways. Written by an authority on word and phrase origins.

Gilbar, Steven, ed. *The Reader's Quotation Book: A Literary Companion,* 2nd ed. Wainscott, N.Y.: Pushcart Press, 1991. Celebrates the reader by collecting hundreds of observations from famous authors on the art of reading. The entries are excellent sentences and paragraphs that should be turned around in the mind slowly.

Goss, Leonard George and Don M. Aycock, eds. *Inside Religious Publishing: A Look Behind the Scenes.* Grand Rapids, Mich.: Zondervan Publishing House, 1991. The publishing scene can be a mystery to people who want to write or otherwise be involved in the field. And religious publishing seems stranger yet. In this book, over thirty experts dispel the mysteries and show a writer how to get started.

Hammond Atlas of the World, 4th ed. Maplewood, N.J.: Hammond, 2002. Many think it is the best atlas.

Harris, William H. and Judith S. Levy. *The New Columbia Encyclopedia,* 4th ed. New York: Columbia University Press, 1980. One of the best single-volume reference volumes an editor can have. Covers the humanities, the life and physical sciences, the social sciences, and geography.

Hayakawa, Samuel I. and Eugene Ehrlich. *Choose the Right Word: A Contemporary Guide to Selecting the Precise Word for Every Situation,* 2nd ed. New York: HarperCollins, 1994. This is a blend of thesaurus, dictionary, and manual of English usage.

Hook, J. N. *The Grand Panjandrum and 2,699 Other Rare, Useful, and Delightful Words and Expressions,* rev. and expanded ed. New York: Collier Books, 1991. All entries are real, existent, useful rare words done in a chapter format (with different subject matter for each chapter) with part of the total list of words presented in alphabetical order within each chapter. The author is a verified verbidopterist.

Horowitz, Lois. *Knowing Where to Look: The Ultimate Guide to Research,* rev. and updated ed. Cincinnati, Ohio: Writer's Digest Books, 1988. This book is a painless approach to using libraries, finding facts, locating rare and unusual sources, avoiding research traps and dead ends, tracking down statistics and quotes, finding answers to quick-and-dirty questions, and much more. An excellent resource for writers and editors.

Horowitz, Lois. *A Writer's Guide to Research.* Cincinnati, Ohio: Writer's Digest Books, 1986. A guide to the quickest way to the information you need as a writer.

Information Please Almanac, Atlas, and Yearbook. New York: Viking Press, annual. A useful and comprehensive chronology of world events.

Into Print: Guides to the Writing Life by the staff of *Poets & Writers Magazine.* New York: National Endowment for the Arts/QPBC, 1995. An excellent and practical resource for writers at all levels offering basic but important information about virtually all aspects of the writing craft, from editorial and contractual matters to how to buy health insurance designed for writers. A collection of the best articles from *Poets & Writers Magazine.*

Kipfer, Barbara Ann (revised by). *Roget's International Thesaurus,* 6th ed. New York: HarperCollins Publishers, 2001. This is the classic thesaurus, compiled according to the plan devised originally by Peter Mark Roget (d. 1869); it is still considered the standard. The text is about 250,000 words and phrases, arranged in more than a thousand categories by their meanings. Also contains a comprehensive index.

Kipfer, Barbara Ann. *Twenty-First Century Synonym and Antonym Finder.* New York: Dell Publishing Company, 1993. More than twenty thousand synonyms and antonyms in an A-to-Z format with preferred usages and spellings.

Korach, Myron and John Mordock. *Common Phrases and Where They Come From.* Guilford, Conn.: The Lyons Press, 2002. The origins of common phrases and colorful expressions.

Landau, Sidney I. *Dictionaries: The Art and Craft of Lexicography,* 2nd ed. New York: Cambridge University Press, 2001. The authoritative source on dictionaries and dictionary making.

Langdon, John. *Wordplay: Ambigrams and Reflections on the Art of Ambigrams.* Orlando, Fla.: Harcourt Brace Jovanovich, Publishers, 1992. A delightful book for lovers of words and art. Ambigrams are words so scripted that they are the same when read upside down, back to front, or in the mirror as well as left to right. Word ambigrams are cousins of picture ambigrams, such as faces that turn into other faces when inverted. The purpose? To present familiar concepts in an unfamiliar way, to stimulate one's imagination, and to see things in a new light.

Lederer, Richard. *Crazy English: The Ultimate Joy Ride Through Our Language,* rev. ed. New York: Pocket Books/Simon & Schuster, 1998. By the author of *Anguished English, Get Thee to a Punnery,* and *The Miracle of Language,* this book is a highly entertaining look at how logic and consistency are often not a part of our language but a crazy randomness is.

Lederer, Richard. *The Miracle of Language,* rev. ed. New York: Pocket Books, 1999. This book is in praise of English. The author calls it "a love letter to the most glorious of human achievements—our ability to utter words, write words, and receive words." Contains a wonderful gallimaufry on words about words for word lovers.

Lewis, C. S. *Studies in Words,* 2nd ed. Cambridge, Eng.: Cambridge University Press, 1967; canto imprint edition 1990. *Studies in Words* explores the nature and implication of language and the theory of meaning by taking a series of words and "teasing out their connotations using examples from a vast range of English literature, recovering lost meanings and analysing their functions." This is a brilliant and entertaining study of the pleasures and problems of verbal communication. The point of view is philological, lexical, historical, and scholarly, and it is as absorbing as all Lewis's writing.

Lighter, J. E., ed. *Random House Historical Dictionary of American Slang.* New York: Random House, 1997. A monumental multivolume dictionary that spans three hundred years of American language history.

Literary Market Place: The Directory of the American Book Publishing Industry. New York: R. R. Bowker Company, updated annually. This is an absolutely thorough listing of publishers, editorial services, agents, book manufacturers, publishing associations, book events, courses, awards, and markets. Massive and the best resource to the entire industry that you can find.

Lovinger, Paul W. *The Penguin Dictionary of American English Usage and Style.* New York: Penguin, 2002. Covers some two thousand examples of misusage.

Luey, Beth. *Handbook for Academic Authors,* 4th ed. New York: Cambridge University Press, 2002. Arizona State University professor Luey takes academicians in hand to show them the business of publishing. Includes guidelines on choosing and approaching a publishing house, preparing scholarly manuscripts, revising and submitting dissertations, contributing to scholarly journals, writing book contracts, seeking permissions, using electronic formats, writing textbooks, and more.

Lutz, William D. *The Cambridge Thesaurus of American English.* New York: Cambridge University Press, 1994. A collection of more than 200,000 synonyms and antonyms for the most commonly used words and phrases in contemporary American English.

McArthur, Tom. *Oxford Guide to World English.* New York: Oxford University Press, 2003. A survey of English as the preeminent world language in its British and American forms as well as an increasingly divergent language.

McCrum, Robert, William Cran, and Robert MacNeil. *The Story of English,* rev. ed. New York: Viking Penguin 1993. The tale of the language that conquered the world and is now spoken by more than a billion people. This book is a popular and entertaining history of the language and a companion to the PBS television series of the same name.

McCutcheon, Marc. *Descriptionary,* 2nd ed. New York: Facts on File, 2000. A thematic dictionary that defines thousands of terms and is organized into more than twenty up-to-date subject categories.

McKean, Evin, ed. *Weird and Wonderful Words*. New York: Oxford University Press, 2002. A collection of hundreds of rare words with many illustrations. A treasury of philological delights.

Merriam-Webster Collegiate Dictionary, 11th ed. Springfield, Mass.: Merriam-Webster, 2003. The eleventh edition is based on a citation file of over 14 million examples of English words. Most publishing houses in the U.S. use this dictionary as their authority on the vocabulary of English, and all editors should have a copy of the most recent edition. It is especially good on capitalization, hyphenation, word division, and guidance on synonyms and usage.

Merriam Webster's Encyclopedia of Literature. Springfield, Mass.: Merriam-Webster, in collaboration with Encyclopedia Britannica, 1995). This comprehensive and authoritative guide combines the best features of a dictionary and an encyclopedia, all focused on the appreciation of the written word. It is an indispensable tool for students, teachers, writers, and editors. There are more than ten thousand entries for authors, works, terms, topics, and movements from all over the world, and it includes coverage of all literary forms, including novels, poems, plays, essays, and literary criticism.

Metter, Ellen. *The Writer's Ultimate Research Guide.* Cincinnati, Ohio: Writer's Digest Books, 1995. Where to find sources of information on many subjects for writers of stories, articles, and books.

Morris, Evan. *The Word Detective: Solving the Mysteries Behind Those Pesky Words and Phrases.* Chapel Hill, N.C.: Algonquin Books, 2000. A feast of word lore.

Neaman, Judith S. and Carole G. Silver. *The Words-worth Book of Euphemism*. Ware, Hertfordshire, Eng.: Wordsworth Editions, 1995. Milder options for crude, embarrassing, and offensive terms.

New International Atlas. New York: Rand McNally, 1999. Another excellent atlas.

Nurnberg, Maxwell. *I Always Look Up the Word "Egregious": A Vocabulary Book for People Who Don't Need One*. Englewood Cliffs, N.J.: Prentice-Hall, 1982. An outstanding manual for people who want to improve their vocabularies. Instructive comments and entertaining anecdotes.

Nuwer, Hank. *How to Write like an Expert About Anything*. Cincinnati, Ohio: Writer's Digest Books, 1995. How to find facts for more interesting and authoritative writing.

Page, G. Terry, comp. *The Wordsworth Book of Spelling Rules*. Ware, Hertfordshire, Eng.: Wordsworth Editions, 1995. First published as *Harrap's English Spelling Rules*, this is a concise self-instruction manual to the sometimes tricky rules of English spelling, with a guideline for spelling improvement.

Partridge, Eric; Paul Beale, ed. *Partridge's Concise Dictionary of Slang and Unconventional English*. New York: Macmillan Publishing Company, 1990. This work is from the 8th ed. (1984) of *A Dictionary of Slang and Unconventional English* by Eric Partridge. Edmund Wilson said "this dictionary . . . is a masterful performance and ought to be acquired by every reader who wants for his library a sound lexicographical foundation."

Pollard, Elaine and Helen Liebeck. *Oxford Paperback Dictionary*, 4th ed. Oxford: Oxford University Press, 1995.

Designed for everyday use with up-to-date vocabulary and definitions.

Randall, Bernice. *When Is a Pig a Hog? A Guide to Confoundingly Related English Words.* New York: Prentice Hall/Simon & Schuster, 1991. The answer is, when it weighs more than 120 pounds. A pig is an immature swine weighing less. Answers hundreds of language questions.

Random House Dictionary of the English Language, 2nd ed. Unabridged. New York: Random House, 1987. Widely respected.

Random House Webster's College Dictionary. New York: Random House, 2000. Good all-purpose dictionary.

Random House Webster's College Thesaurus. New York: Random House, 1998. Each synonym is introduced in a sample sentence. This thesaurus uses the alphabetical arrangement.

The Random House Webster's Unabridged Dictionary. New York: Random House, 2001. Taken from *The Random House Dictionary of the English Language.*

Rodale, J. I.; rev. by Laurence Urdang, et al. *The Synonym Finder,* rev. ed. Emmaus, Penn.: Rodale Press, 1978. This has over one million synonyms and makes a marvelous companion for writers, editors, speakers, students, and teachers. The book abounds, teems, flourishes, overflows with helpful entries.

Room, Adrian. *Brewer's Dictionary of Modern Phrase & Fable.* Portland, Ore.: Cassell Academic, 2001. Shows the rich and diverse linguistic and cultural landscape of the modern world. Informative and highly entertaining.

Schur, Norman W. *Practical English: 1000 Most Effective Words,* reissue ed. New York: Ballantine Books, 1988. For all who want to use common words correctly.

Shaw, Harry. *Dictionary of Problem Words and Expressions,* rev. ed. New York: McGraw-Hill Book Company, 1987. An alphabetical arrangement of problem words and expressions are described, discussed, and illustrated with examples from actual usage. Will alert readers to faulty writing habits.

Sheehy, Eugene Paul. *Guide to Reference Books,* 10th ed. Chicago: American Library Association, 1986. Recommends the basic reference materials available throughout the world, with excellent annotated listings. A tremendous range of sources for quick fact-finding.

Shipley, Joseph T. *Playing with Words.* Englewood Cliffs, N.J.: Prentice-Hall, 1983. Word games, semantic antics, rhymes, and puns.

Silva, Moises. *Biblical Words and Their Meaning: An Introduction to Lexical Semantics,* rev. ed. Grand Rapids, Mich.: Academie Books, Zondervan Publishing House, 1995. A thorough, up-to-date exposition of the nature of biblical lexicology.

Skeat, Walter W. *A Concise Etymological Dictionary of the English Language.* New York: Oxford University Press, 1996. Originally published in 1882. Still famous and valuable for all wishing to discover the origins of words. The word list contains primary words of most frequent occurrence, as well as others prominent in literature.

Soukhanov, Anne. *Word Watch: The Stories Behind the Words of Our Lives.* New York: Henry Holt and Company,

1995. From affluenza to zip code wine, this book covers the origins of intriguing words that make a statement about our society.

Spears, Richard A. *Slang and Euphemism,* 3rd ed. New York: Signet, 2001. A dictionary of oaths, insults, slang and metaphor, slurs, drug lingo, and related matters. A good reference for usually prohibited words and subjects.

Stein, Jeff and Laurence Urdang. *The Random House Basic Dictionary of Synonyms and Antonyms,* 2nd ed. New York: Ballantine Books, 1991. Over eighty thousand words listed. Great for writers, editors, and speakers.

Sydnor, William. *More Than Words.* San Francisco: Harper & Row, Publishers, 1990. This is a dictionary for professional and lay religious leaders, teachers, editors, and others involved in religious education, offering clear and concise definitions on terminology relating to the Christian faith. The book amounts to a primer on Christianity and provides insight, Scripture references, and illustrations.

The Times Atlas of the World, comprehensive 10th ed. New York: Times Books, 1999. An outstanding and massive atlas.

Train, John. *Valsalva's Maneuver: Mots Justes and Indispensable Terms.* New York: HarperCollins, 1990. The author himself describes this funny and essential little handbook as a guide to "elegant word-dropping." As for Valsalva's maneuver, it is when one holds one's nose and blows out one's cheeks in an elevator or airplane to relieve pressure in the ears.

Tripp, Roda Thomas, comp. *The International Thesaurus of Quotations,* reprint ed. New York: HarperCollins, 1987.

One of the most useful books of quotations you can have. Look for an idea closest to your own thought, and you will find many quotations to put that thought into appropriate words. Arranged alphabetically.

United States Government Organizational Manual. Washington, D.C.: U.S. Government Printing Office, annual. Updated annually, this book gives background information on each of the government's various agencies, quasi-agencies, bureaus, offices, and commissions. It has a list of names, addresses, and phone numbers of the press officers of those agencies.

Urdang, Laurence, ed. *The New York Times Everyday Reader's Dictionary of Misunderstood, Misused, Mispronounced Words,* rev. ed. New York: Quadrangle Books, 1991. Interesting and unusual words with their definitions, but lacking advice on their usage.

Varchaver, Mary and Frank Ledlie Moore. *The Browser's Dictionary of Foreign Words and Phrases.* Hoboken, N.J.: John Wiley & Sons, 2001. The pronunciations, definitions, and derivations of 2,000 words from Greek, Latin, French, Russian, Hindi, Gaelic, Japanese, and other languages, with examples of their use in current English.

Webster's New Dictionary of Synonyms: A Dictionary of Discriminated Synonyms with Antonyms and Analogous and Contrasted Words, 2nd ed. Springfield, Mass.: Merriam-Webster, 1984. Every word discussed in an article is entered into its own alphabetical place, followed by a list of synonyms, and most often attended by quotations from classic as well as contemporary writers to illustrate their meanings.

Webster's New Explorer Dictionary of Synonyms and

Antonyms. New York: Federal Street Press, 2003. Useful guide to thousands of synonyms and antonyms.

Webster's New Geographical Dictionary, rev. ed. Springfield, Mass.: Merriam-Webster, 1988. Handy reference for place-names, alternative names, and former names.

Webster's New World Basic Dictionary of American English, by the staff of Webster's New World Dictionary. New York: John Wiley & Sons, 1998. A basic dictionary of almost fifty thousand commonly used words in the American English lexicon. Especially useful for beginners in English reading and speaking.

Webster's New World Dictionary of the American Language, 3rd ed. New York: Warner Books, 1991. Noted for its sharp and concise definitions.

Webster's New World Pocket Biographical Dictionary. Springfield, Mass.: Merriam-Webster, 1994. Short biographies of nonliving persons. Excellent for quickly checking names, dates, spellings, and other factual information.

Webster's Third New International Dictionary of the English Language, unabridged. Springfield, Mass.: Merriam-Webster, 2002. 500,000 entries, with 3,000 pictures. Extensive, comprehensive, and authoritative. Especially good reference for new words. May be the best unabridged dictionary.

Wentworth, Harold and Robert L. Chapman, comp. *Dictionary of American Slang,* 3rd ed. New York: HarperCollins Publishers, 1998. A vast number of entries on regionalisms and colloquialisms, with thousands of slang definitions from many different times and places (politics, entertainment, jazz, the underworld, the armed forces, business, teenagers, the sports world, the beat generation, and more).

Word Mysteries and Histories: From Quiche to Humble Pie, by the editors of The American Heritage Dictionaries. Boston: Houghton Mifflin Company, 1987. Intriguing and sometimes whimsical facts about the backgrounds of more than five hundred English words.

The World Almanac and Book of Facts 2003. New York: World Almanac Education, 2002. A chronology of each year's world events reported on many different fields.

C. Book Editing

Berg, Scott. *Max Perkins: Editor of Genius.* New York: Riverhead Books, 1997. A moving biography of a great editor, full of interesting background on the book trade. Some of the literary careers Perkins nourished at Scribners were those of Fitzgerald, Hemingway, Thomas Wolfe, Sherwood Anderson, and Taylor Caldwell.

Boston, Bruce O. *Language on a Leash.* Alexandria, Va.: Editorial Experts, 1988. Interesting collection of essays examining the nuances of writing, editing, usage, and the English language.

Boston, Bruce O., ed. *STET Again: More Tricks of the Trade for Publications People.* Alexandria, Va.: Editorial Experts, 1996. This book collects invaluable articles from The Editorial Eye, a magazine focusing on publications standards and practices. The material falls into separate topics—editing (on being an editor, special editorial problems, the levels of edit), writing (tools for writers, the writers' craft, plain English), publications management (running the shop, productivity standards, production), indexing, proofreading, lexicography, and the finer points of spelling, punctuation, and usage.

Butcher, Judith M. *Copy-Editing: The Cambridge Handbook Desk Edition,* 3rd ed. New York: Cambridge University Press, 1991. Handles the whole range of editorial processes necessary to move from the text or disk to the printed page. Many excellent checklists and examples.

Chaplin, Joyce. *Writers, My Friends.* Colorado Springs: David C. Cook, 1984. This monograph challenges editors and publishers to be active in encouraging and training Christian writers in the developing world. The personal and editorial advice Chaplin shares in this material will help all who counsel new writers.

Cheney, Theodore A. Rees. *Getting the Words Right: How to Rewrite, Edit & Revise,* reprint ed. Cincinnati, Ohio: Writer's Digest Books, 1990. The secret to all good writing is revision. This book shows how one can improve anything one writes by three editing revision techniques: reduction, rearranging, and rewording.

Commins, Dorothy Berliner. *What Is an Editor? Saxe Commins at Work.* Chicago: University of Chicago Press, 1978. An unusually good survey of the publishing process by looking at one of the outstanding literary editors of Random House who influenced such personalities as Dreiser, Faulkner, O'Neill, Michener, and many others.

Dillard, Annie. *The Writing Life,* reprint ed. New York: HarperPerennial, 1999. A wonderful window through which the writing process is viewed. This will benefit any writer, but it will also help editors understand their writers.

Directory of Editorial Resources. Compiled by the staff of Editorial Experts. Alexandria, Va.: Editorial Experts, 1990. A compendium of information for professional editors.

Gross, Gerald, ed. *Editors on Editing: What Writers Need to Know About What Editors Do,* 3rd ed. New York: Grove Press, 1993. A superb collection of essays from industry insiders to help writers (as well as editors) understand editing at its best. All writers, editors, publishers, and agents should have this.

Harman, Eleanor and Ian Montagnes, ed. *The Thesis and the Book.* Toronto: University of Toronto Press, 1983. The real differences between a thesis or dissertation and a publishable book are explored by six contributors who are editors, publishers, and scholars. Careful attention to this book will result in improved academic writing.

Henderson, Bill ed. *The Art of Literary Publishing: Editors on Their Craft,* reprint ed. Wainscott, N.Y.: Pushcart Press, 1995. Articles from professional editors, many well-known in the field.

Howry, Michelle. *Agents, Editors, and You.* Cincinnati, Ohio: Writer's Digest Books, 2002. The insider's guide to getting your book published.

Judd, Karen. *Copyediting: A Practical Guide,* 3rd ed. Los Altos, Calif.: Crisp Publications, 2001. A lively manual full of professional advice and examples for editors at all stages. Goes from the basics through the bibliography and gives a good overview of the copy editor's role in the publishing process.

Lamott, Anne. *Bird by Bird: Some Instructions on Writing and Life.* New York: Pantheon Books, 1994. What does it take to be a writer? What does it *mean* to be a writer? A funny, personal, and inspiring step-by-step guide on how to write and manage a writer's life.

Leax, John. *Grace Is Where I Live: Writing as a Christian Vocation.* Grand Rapids, Mich.: Baker Books, 1993. A poet's reflections on life lived as a writer and the serious questions Christians who choose the vocation of writing must ask. Has a clear relevance for editors and publishers also.

Lerner, Betsy. *The Forest for the Trees: An Editor's Advice to Writers.* New York: Riverhead Books, 2000. Writing and book publishing from an editor's point of view, from the ecstasy of acquisition to the agony of the remainder table.

Lukeman, Noah T. *The First Five Pages: A Writer's Guide to Staying Out of the Rejection Pile.* New York: Fireside, 2000. A literary agent teaches how to identify and avoid bad writing. Covers presentation, pacing, and progression and includes writing exercises.

Mandell, Judy. *Book Editors Talk to Writers.* New York: John Wiley & Sons, 1995. Addressed to writers and based on interviews with forty-four professional editors. Covers many important areas of interest, such as queries and proposals, publishing lingo, agents, how publishing decisions are made, editor-author etiquette and relations, and book packaging.

May, Rollo. *The Courage to Create.* New York: W.W. Norton and Company, 1994. A famous therapist observes the process of creativity and helps us in our search for creative possibilities. May finds that people express their being by creating and that the apprehension of beauty is a road to truth.

McCormack, Thomas. *The Fiction Editor.* New York: St. Martin's Press, 1988. A superb essay on the art and craft of editing fiction.

McHugh, John B. *Managing Book Acquisitions: An Introduction.* Glendale, Wis.: John B. McHugh, 1995. An overview of the entire process of finding and recruiting authors and acquiring books.

Merriam Webster's Manual for Writers and Editors. Springfield, Mass.: Merriam-Webster, Inc., 1998. An authoritative guide to writing rules and procedures covering a broad range of topics encountered by writers and editors in all subjects and all kinds of publications.

Molpus, Ann R., ed. *The Expert Editor: Tips, Advice, Insights, and Solutions.* Alexandria, Va. Editorial Experts, 1991. Editorial Experts, an editorial consulting firm, covers many different areas, including setting productivity standards, maintaining editorial integrity, editing "prima donna" authors, and developing writers' guidelines.

Nichols, Sue. *Words on Target for Better Christian Communication.* Louisville: John Knox Press, 1988. A handy book showing how to avoid the danger spots in religious writing.

Norris, Kathleen. *Dakota: A Spiritual Geography.* Boston: Ticknor & Fields/Houghton Mifflin Company, 2001. A sensitive, spiritual, and deeply moving book of "good telling stories" occasioned when a writer from New York and her poet-husband return to her family tradition on the Great Plains (in Lemmon, South Dakota) to find her geographical and cultural identity and to build her own traditions and pursue her vocation as a writer. Dakota shows the meaning of inheritance and how the power of words can effect change in the human heart.

Plotnik, Arthur. *The Elements of Editing: A Modern Guide for Editors and Journalists.* New York: Macmillan Publishing Company, 1996. A fun-to-read, informal guide in the tradition of Strunk and White's *The Elements of Style* and an inside look at editing and editorial advice. Writers and editors should have this.

Rabiner, Susan and Alfred Fortunato. *Thinking like Your Editor.* New York: W. W. Norton, 2002. For nonfiction writers who need help getting published.

See, Carolyn. *Making a Literary Life.* New York: Ballantine Books, 2003. Advice for writers and other dreamers.

Sharpe, Leslie T. and Irene Gunther. *Editing Fact and Fiction.* New York: Cambridge University Press, 1994. A lively and concise overview of the many opportunities in the editing field and the different kinds of book editing, meant both for those who think they want to get into editing and those already working in it.

Stainton, Elsie Myers. *Author and Editor at Work: Making a Better Book.* Toronto: University of Toronto Press, 1982. Knowing what may cause problems for an editor is important information for authors, and vice versa.

Stein, Sol. *Stein on Writing.* New York: St. Martin's Griffin, 2000. Solutions to just about any writing problem one may encounter from a successful novelist and literary editor.

Stoughton, Mary. *Substance and Style: Instruction and Practice in Copyediting,* rev. Alexandria, Va.: Editorial Experts, 1996. A self-teaching manual full of exercises and examples.

Unseld, Siegfried; Hunter Hannum and Hildegarde Hannum, trans. *The Author and His Publisher.* Chicago: The University of Chicago Press, 1980. The author writes about the author-publisher relationship. He closely examines four writers (Hermann Hesse, Bertolt Brecht, Rainer Maria Rilke, and Robert Walser) and their publishers and shows that the author's personality can affect the publisher's reaction.

Van Buren, Robert and Mary Fran Buehler. *The Levels of Edit,* 2nd ed. Pasadena, Calif.: Jet Propulsion Laboratory, California Institute of Technology, 1992. Useful in the field of technical communication. This brief book analyzes the editorial process and identifies five levels of edit that are cumulative combinations of nine types of edit: coordination, policy, integrity, screening, copy clarification, format, mechanical style, language, and substantive.

Wheelock, John Hall, ed. *Editor to Author: The Letters of Maxwell E. Perkins,* reprint ed. New York: Charles Scribner's Sons, 1997. Letters to his authors from one of the greatest literary editors of all time. Instructive for all editors.

D. Computers, Electronic Editing, Databases, and Computer Networking

Banks, Michael. *The Modem Reference,* 4th ed. New York: Simon & Schuster, 2000. Excellent textbook on telecomputing, describing and explaining modems, communication software packages, bulletin board services, research databases, electronic mail, online services, and much more.

Chicago Guide to Preparing Electronic Manuscripts for Authors and Publishers. Chicago: University of Chicago

Press, 1987. This is somewhat dated, but it is still an excellent reference tool for writers and editors covering most aspects of preparing manuscripts in electronic form for submission to a publisher.

The Columbia Guide to Digital Publishing. New York: Columbia University Press, 2003. "The first reference work to bring together every facet of the digital publishing process in one unique, accessible resource."

Fluegelman, Andrew and Jeremy Joan Hewes. *Writing in the Computer Age: Word Processing Skills and Style for Every Writer.* Garden City, N.Y.: Anchor Books/Doubleday & Company, 1983. An older but valuable guide to computers for writers that covers hardware and software, electronic file systems, screen and print formatting, editing on a word processor, designing manuscripts, systems linking, and more.

Hedtke, John V. *Using Computer Bulletin Boards,* 2nd ed. New York: Diane Publishing, 1999. How to access bulletin boards.

Lingham, Gretchen, Jim Kimble, and Tina Berke. *How to Get Started with Modems,* 2nd ed. San Diego, Calif.: Computer Publishing Enterprises, 1992. A beginner's guide to modems, electronic bulletin boards, and online services.

McHugh, John B. *Electronic Rights for Publishers: Protecting Your Interests.* Glendale, Wis.: John B. McHugh, 1995. A brief introduction to how publishers can and should protect their electronic rights in the context of today's rapidly evolving field of electronic publishing.

Shillingsburg, Peter L. *Scholarly Editing in the Computer Age: Theory and Practice,* 3rd ed. Ann Arbor: University of Michigan Press, 1996. Looks at the theoretical foundations of scholarly editions, explores the needs of scholars and critics, and suggests ways that computer technology can make it easier and economically more feasible to do scholarly books.

Standera, Oldrich. *The Electronic Era of Publishing: An Overview of Concepts, Technologies, and Methods.* New York: Elsevier, 1987. A good introduction to the conceptual questions on electronic publishing confronting writers and publishers.

Walter, Russ. *The Secret Guide to Computers,* 28th ed. Somerville, Mass.: Russ Walter, 2002. Everything you always wanted to know about computers, including buying hardware and software. Authoritative and complete.

E. Proofreading

Butcher, Judith M. *Typescripts, Proofs and Indexes.* New York: Cambridge University Press, 1980. A brief handbook.

Smith, Debra A. and Helen R. Sutton. *Powerful Proofreading Skills: Tips, Techniques and Tactics.* Normal, Ill.: Crisp Publications, 1995. Helpful to the beginning proofreader, including workbook sections, proofreaders marks, and proofreading strategies.

Smith, Peggy. *Mark My Words: Instruction and Practice in Proofreading,* 3rd ed. Alexandria, Va.: Editorial Experts, 1997. The author offers many exercises in this self-teaching manual on proofreading techniques.

Smith, Peggy. *Proofreading Manual and Reference Guide.* Alexandria, Va.: Editorial Experts, 1981. This is a course textbook and individual instructional manual or refresher course on the techniques of proofreading. It covers all the standard editorial marks and how and when to use them, and also provides the important background that proofreaders need to know to understand their role in the publishing process.

Sullivan, K. D. *Go Ahead, Proof It!* Hauppauge, N.Y.: Barrons Educational Series, 1996. Easy to use guide for the nonprofessional. Shows how to use an editorial style sheet.

F. Indexing

Collision, Robert L. *Indexes and Indexing: Guide to the Indexing of Books*. Tuckahoe, N.Y.: John de Graff, 1972. An overview of the concepts that have to be mastered in preparing a comprehensive index.

Mulvang, Nancy C. *Indexing Books (Chicago Guides to Writing, Editing, and Publishing)*. Chicago: University of Chicago Press, 1994. This expands on standard discussions with analysis and judgment on what to include and exclude from the index and how indexing fits into the publishing industry.

Spiker, Sina and Thomas Webb. *Indexing Your Book: A Practical Guide for Authors,* 2nd ed. Madison, Wis.: The University of Wisconsin Press, 1987. A small manual full of excellent help on assembling index items, analyzing those items, arranging the index, and preparing the copy. Additional material on indexing with computers.

Wellisch, Hans. *Indexing from A to Z,* 2nd ed. New York: H. H. Wilson, 1997. Wonderful resource for anyone, at any stage, in the preparing of indexes. Arranged by topics.

G. Copyright and Literary Law

Ashley, Paul P. *Say It Safely: Legal Limits in Publishing, Radio, and Television.* Seattle, Wash.: University of Washington Press, 1976. An accessible yet thorough explanation of libel law.

Balkin, Richard. *A Writer's Guide to Contract Negotiations.* Cincinnati, Ohio: Writer's Digest Books, 1989. A guide to negotiating specific processes for book and magazine contracts. Good advice from a literary agent on understanding what all the contract clauses really mean, and which are negotiable and which are not.

Brown, Ralph S. and Robert C. Denicola. *Cases on Copyright: Unfair Competition, and Related Topics Bearing on the Protection of Literary, Musical, and Artistic Works.* New York: Foundation Press, 1998. Primarily for lawyers. Contains actual case findings.

Bunnin, Brad and Peter Beren. *Author Law & Strategies.* Berkeley, Calif.: Nolo Press, 1983. An outstanding guide for the working writer. All areas of literary law are covered.

Bunnin, Brad and Peter Beren. *The Writer's Legal Companion.* Reading, Mass.: Addison-Wesley Publishing Company, 1988. A practical nonjargony guide to contracts, copyright, libel, and much more.

Clark, Charles. *Publishing Agreements: A Book of Precedents,* 3rd ed. Boston: George Allen & Unwin, 1990. An authoritative and practical guide through copyright matters. Valuable new precedents have been added—for film, television, packaging rights, reprographic reproduction, electronic publishing, and more. The author has worked as an attorney and legal editor.

Copyright Law of the United States of America. Washington, D.C.: United States Copyright Office of the Library of Congress, 2002. "The copyright law of the United States of America printed herein is the Act for the General Revision of the Copyright Law, Chapters 1 through 8 of Title 17 of the United States Code, together with Transitional and Supplementary Provisions, enacted as Pub. L. 94-553, 90 Stat. 2451, on October 19, 1976."

Crawford, Ted. *The Writer's Legal Guide,* 3rd ed. New York: Allworth Press, 2002. Easy-to-use guide for understanding the legal aspects of publishing, negotiating contracts, and more.

Du Boff, Leonard D. *Book Publishers' Legal Guide.* Redmond, Wash.: Butterworth Legal Publishers, 1987. The business, accounting, copyright, contracts, censorship, rights, suppliers, and trade practices side of publishing.

How to Use the Federal FOI Act. Washington, D.C.: FOI Service Center, 1125 15th Street, N.W., 20005. Have you ever wondered how to take advantage of the Freedom of Information Act? This book will tell you how.

Hurst, Walter E. *Copyright: How to Register Your Copyright and Introduction to New and Historical Copyright Law.* Hollywood, Calif.: Seven Arts Press, 1977. This book informs authors, songwriters, photographers, artists, and others how to do many practical things concerning copyright notice and how not to lose their rights and economic opportunities through ignorance of the copyright laws. The book, however, is dated on new copyright interpretations.

Johnston, Donald F. *Copyright Handbook,* 2nd ed. New York: R. R. Bowker Company, 1982. Thoroughly explaining the new copyright law of 1976 and its complexities, this is designed to offer a general understanding of the law and to provide an accessible format where specific information can be easily found.

Kirsch, Jonathan. *Kirsch's Guide to the Book Contract for Authors, Publishers, Editors and Agents.* Los Angeles: Acrobat Books, 1998. Useful in understanding the important issues involved in publishing contracts.

Kirsch, Jonathan. *Kirsch's Handbook of Publishing Law.* Los Angeles: Acrobat Books, 1995. Written by a lawyer and an expert in literary law, intellectual property matters, and the publishing industry. Uses examples from leading publishing cases. This book is an indispensable quick access yet comprehensive resource covering the full range of legal issues in publishing—idea protection, book development, contracts, electronic rights, multimedia rights, avoiding lawsuits, etc., and legal definitions of such areas as defamation, invasion of privacy, copyright, and trademark.

Madison, Charles A. *Irving to Irving: Author-Publisher Relations, 1800–1974.* New York: R. R. Bowker, 1974. Specific cases that show the evolution of publishing contracts, copyright agreements, and other legal arrangements between writers and their publishers.

Mallon, Thomas. *Stolen Words: Forays into the Origins and Ravages of Plagiarism,* reprint ed. New York: Penguin, 1991. Fascinating accounts of the crime of plagiarism.

McHugh, John B. *Book Publishing Contracts: An Introduction.* Glendale, Wis.: John B. McHugh, 1996. Shows how to negotiate with authors and agents, how to train new acquisitions editors, how to review and revise current contracts, how to understand the why's behind contracts, and other skills. Also gives insights into how the book contract is used as an acquisitions tool.

McHugh, John B. *Permissions Management for Requesters and Granters: Dealing with Copyright and Fair Use.* Glendale, Wis.: John B. McHugh, 1996. A how-to approach for managing the process of permissions for both the requester and the granter.

Newitt, George B. and Janet M. McNicholas. *Answers to Common Questions of Publishers on U.S. Copyright Law.* Chicago: Allegretti & Witcoff, Ltd., n.d. Handles questions related to registration and ownership, the scope of copyright protection, and international protection, as well as copyright notice questions, copying and fair use matters, and questions related to dispute resolution.

Newitt, George B. and Janet M. McNicholas. *A Primer for Book Editors on U.S. Copyright Law.* Chicago: Allegretti & Witcoff, Ltd., n.d. Outline notes that cover the subject matter and scope of copyright, the Berne Convention Implementation Act of 1988, and the Visual Artist Rights Act of 1990.

The Nuts and Bolts of Copyright. Washington, D.C.: United States Government Printing Office, 1978. An official summary of the law.

Owen, Lynette. *Selling Rights,* 4th ed. New York: Routlege, 2001. For those involved in the sale of rights and all other copyright and licensing questions. A comprehensive step-by-step guide to all aspects of selling rights and coeditions, an explanation of the nature of rights that can be granted, and advice on how to get the best possible deal.

Patterson, L. Ray and Stanley W. Lindberg. *The Nature of Copyright: A Law of Users' Rights*. Athens, Ga.: The University of Georgia Press, 1991. Offers a new perspective on copyright law and the legal rights of copyrighted material. The authors warn against accepting inflated claims for copyright protection that are based on misunderstandings of the origin, the purpose, and the meaning of the nature of copyright.

Pinkerton, Linda F. *The Writer's Law Primer*. New York: Lyons & Burford, Publishers, 1990. A good guide to "preventive law" for writers who encounter legal issues, whether they be writers of books, novels, screenplays, texts, articles, or computer programs. The author, an attorney, covers copyright law, author's rights, First Amendment issues, contracts, business considerations (taxes, insurance, noms de plume, etc.), lawsuits, and more.

Polking, Kirk and Leonard S. Meranus. *Law and the Writer*. Cincinnati, Ohio: Writer's Digest books, 1985. Addresses all the questions for the legal problems writers encounter.

Strong, William S. *The Copyright Book: A Practical Guide,* 5th ed. Cambridge, Mass.: MIT Press, 1999. The best brief introduction to copyright law and how it is applied.

Wincor, Richard. *Literary Rights Contracts: A Handbook for Professionals*. New York: Harcourt Brace Jovanovich, 1979. Most useful for lawyers, literary agents, and publishing personnel dealing with contracts.

Wittenberg, Philip. *The Protection of Literary Property,* 2nd rev. ed. Boston: The Writer, 1978. Explores the laws and regulations on copyright from the new copyright legislation.

CHAPTER 13
Subject Index

About the Authors

Leonard G. Goss is editorial director, Trade and Academic Book Publishing, Broadman & Holman Publishers. Before coming to B&H, Len was the editorial vice president at Crossway Books and imprint editor at Zondervan Publishing House. He began his publishing career with the firm John Wiley & Sons. He is active on a national scale as a public speaker on writing, editing, and publishing. Len is coauthor of *Writing Religiously* and *The Christian Writer's Book* and coeditor of *Inside Religious Publishing,* and he has contributed chapters to many different books.

Carolyn Stanford Goss graduated with high distinction from Arizona State University and received the master's degree from Vanderbilt University. She has extensive experience in publishing, having worked in marketing and special sales for Random House, Richard D. Irwin, and McGraw-Hill. Carolyn currently does freelance copywriting and editing, tutors English as a second language, and teaches composition and literature at Williamson Christian College and reading at Columbia State Community College. She is also the author of *Skills for Success,* a modular life and study skills curriculum used by the Consortium of Online Christian Colleges.